Endorsements

It has been an honor to watch the Science of Miracles unfold in my friend and colleague Dr. Sharnael's life. I first met this incredible woman in 2009 and watched her manifest miracles in her career, time and time again. Later in 2014 we developed a dear friendship where I would get an up close and personal seat in her walk of "RE-Membering the Frequency of Love." Miracle after miracle happened and the foundation of the Science of Miracles was born.

In 2018, I found myself in a state of depression. I would cry every day, fear and anxiety plagued me, and the simplest decisions overwhelmed me. Then God called me to Dr. Sharnael's "*The Science of Miracles... RE-Membering The Frequency of Love.*" I studied the material over and over again for two weeks and applied what I learned. Quickly, miraculous doors opened up in my life, solutions to unsolvable problems, and abundant blessings came in. I found my Joy, Love, Peace and Passion for life again!

If you want more Love, Joy, Peace and Miracles in your life then learn how to Re-Member the Frequency of Love and you will have the Science of Miracles in your life too!

Dr. Mary Starr Carter
The Total Wellness Doc and Mom
TheTotalWellnessDoc.com

* * *

Awareness is the beginning of Living True. Through Dr. Sharnael's personal stories and scientific research, she validates all! As you read this book, you are Divinely timed for your highest good and waking up to a new future of creative manifestation. Thoughts are the language of the brain and feelings are the language of the body. When we align in love, miracles upon miracles and the art of fulfillment are ours!

Dr. Marcella Vonn Harting, PhD
MarcellaVonnHarting.com

* * *

Vibrant health is not only about the food you eat and the exercise you do, it is also about the way you think—and your mindset. How you think determines how you act. "The Science of Miracles" is a book that provides us all with the tools to help us RE-Member that what we think, feel and talk about matters. This is a book you will want to read and re-read many times.

Dr. Pia Martin DC, CCN, CWC, CHC
Best Selling Author of *Building Healthy Humans*
DrPia.com

* * *

As a practicing Transformational Physician for 20 years, I have noted the hallmark of a good author, teacher, and leader is to be able to present complex information in a simple manner that even a child could understand. Dr. Sharnael does an excellent job de-cluttering the deception in our lives that hinder us from reaching our highest levels spiritually, emotionally, and physically. Over the years I have known Dr. Sharnael to be the leader who knows the way, shows the way, and goes the way.

Einstein's formula of $E=mc^2$ reveals that everything is energy (frequency). Even humans are beings of light. And, like Christ, we are spirit robed in flesh. In this book, Dr. Sharnael skillfully unmasks the spirit and light in us so we can have the necessary shift within ourselves to possess the miracles we so deeply desire.

Thomas Lucky MD, P(MD)
Unleashing the Healing Miracle Within
TheFlowClinic.com

* * *

Dr. Sharnael is the "Real Deal." My Sister of Light practices everything she shares and shares everything she experiences on her Path of Spirit. She deeply applies any truth or what I call 'Laws of Life' and integrates her experiences and understandings with her vast study of Scripture, Science, Quantum Physics, and Life in such a way as to engage TRUTH fully. I listen to her sharing and what she may have learned, as she always amplifies what she learns. She is very present and committed to Truth and she raises others by her experience.

I consider Dr. Sharnael a Master Teacher, Inspirer, Leader, Doer, and Servant of Our Creator on every level. As I read this book in its early form, I immediately was, and AM, thrilled to dive deeply into the material for myself. One special thing about "Real Deal" Spiritual Teachers for me is they manifest miracles consistently. This is Dr. Sharnael Wolverton Sehon.

Robert Tennyson Stevens
Author of *Conscious Language*™
MasterySystems.com

* * *

What a beautiful harmony of science and Spirit! Scripture says, "The thing that hath been, it is that which shall be; and that which is done is that which shall be done: and there is no new thing under the sun." (Eccl. 1:9, KJV). And so, we have the wisdom of Spirit manifesting in this beautiful work, re-emerging into our ready time. Dr. Sharnael has taken the mystification and superstition out of many of the misunderstood realities that surround us, and made it into an easy to understand book based on the spiritual and physical laws of God. Full of interesting insights as well as a practical guide.

David Stewart, PhD
Author of *Healing Oils of The Bible*
RaindropTraining.com

The Science of Miracles

RE-Membering the Frequency of Love

By Dr. Sharnael Wolverton Sehon

For more information about our products or services, please visit our website or contact:
www.swiftfire.org or www.drsharnael.com
Dr. Sharnael Wolverton Sehon
sharnael@swiftfire.org

Swiftfire Publishing

Publishers Cataloging-in-Publication Data
Keto Reset.; by Sharnael Wolverton Sehon
148 pages cm.
ISBN: 9780979662263 paperbook
      9780979662270 eBook
      9780979662287 eBook
Printed in the United States of America

Dedication

This book is dedicated to you.

You all made this possible for me.

I have several amazing people I am so forever thankFull to: my Creator,
my parents Chris and Connie, my Divine Love—Brian and my beautiFULL kiddos,
Shaen & Austin, Søren, Ava, Sharnael and Adam.

I am thankful for my many teachers:
Bob Jones, John Paul Jackson, Dr. Thomas Lucky,
Dr. David Stewart, Dr. Gary and Mary Young, Dr. Marcella Vonn Harting,
Robert Tennyson Stevens and several others over the years.

To my GGs, my "wake up" besties, you know who you are… I thank my team.

Thank you ALL for helping me RE-Member Love Now.

I not only thank all of you for your love and support in the actual writing of
this book, but the literal support THROUGH the experiences that shifted me to
even be on the planet and experience these things to even write about them.

You ALL mean more than any words could ever say.

To everyone who made this possible.

Thank you, Marti Statler. You are truly an angel sent to me.
Thank you Shannon Johnson, Christal Washington, and
Colleen Higgs for jumping in to help!

Thank you, Trezher. What would I do without you?

To everyone who has followed and supported me over the years, whether on
social media, my classes, conferences, etc. on this journey over,
in, and through all our transformation together all through the years.

You are *my people* and I adore you.

I AM Already Loved and my Love Stays,

Xoxo
Dr. Sharnael

Table of Contents

Preface

You can't pee in the pool and hope it doesn't get EVERYwhere.

By the same token—"smoking sections" at restaurants—it is ridiculous to separate them from the rest of the dining area because it is obvious that smoke gets everywhere (eye roll).

With energy it is the same thing. If you have any "issues," negative energy or low frequency in one area of your life, issues exist in ALL areas of your life. Energy doesn't categorize your business in one section, your love life to another, and your health over yonder; it just is. It's ALL YOU. I mean, YOU are all YOU.

It's funny, a bit before the time I actually started really "waking up," I had this intense longing to move back home to Montana where I was born. It was such a heartache... I literally felt it in the morning, all day until I went to bed. This really, really intense feeling in my heart; an empty feeling... I just knew I had to be "back home." I didn't realize until later was that it wasn't "home" as in *Montana* that I was missing, it was ME home.

I was missing me.

I was missing the 'fun me' that didn't worry about all the things that had me worried at the time: bills, people, relationships, and those stupid negative patterns that played on a continuous loop in my mind. Those patterns were taking up way too much energy, and way too much headspace.

I was missing the kid who painted, and wrote songs and poetry, and played with animals **outside**.

The chick who created, sang, had fun with her friends, enjoyed life, lived in the moment, who loved nature and flowers and mountains and grass and picnics and flying kites and beaches, belly laughing and reading and just having smiley days.

That was when I started "waking up" and *seeing* everything had to change. I had to be "Me" again... IN me. "Home." The only way real change would happen permanently was from the inside out. Everything has to start as an INSIDE job. I ONLY get what I am, and I get to CREATE with EASE AND JOY AND FUN... things shifted very rapidly and, in some cases, INSTANTLY.

There truly is **NO PLACE LIKE HOME**.

It truly is an **INSIDE JOB**.

You can do anything from the inside out... starting with you/me/us... just like I did and continue to do.

We get to do some amazing stuff here on earth and we get to create our lives.... You are **already** creating one way or another **anyway**... Why not create cool stuff while you are at it? Why not make it fun and easy?

You've most likely heard the saying, "go big or go home!"

Well I say...

"Stay home and go BIG."

As you read this, I encourage you to simply apply it, as your life begins to walk the fun path of Miracles.

Chapter 1

Let Me Help You Turn the Lights On!

YOU DESERVE A LIFE OF MIRACLES. The Spirit, Quantum Physics and the Supernatural are amazing. God is the biggest Scientist of us all. I invite you to reconcile God within the ideas that I share in this book. Even if it sounds 'freaky' to you... bear with me. To be honest, a lot of things I experienced were scary at first too. I had some doubt, it seemed weird, and in all actuality, I thought at times, *"This is sketchy, and a little too 'woo-woo' for me."* But on the other side... now... after reverse-engineering it all, I am *seeing* and more importantly, *experiencing* the positive results. AND guess what? I know I can help you too, and hopefully even save you from making any of the idiotic choices I once made.

I've been aware of Spirit for almost 43 years now, and what I'm really RE-Membering[a] and dis-covering as I am open to Truth, and RE-Membering Truth, and Being True, is that oils, food, crystals, people, nature, emotions, words, music, and much more, all have frequency. There are a ton of scriptures that support that, too. Through my education and experiences, I have RE-Membered these things I will share with you in this book. And I am a work in progress.

---

a   RE- means to do again and STAY. Membered is to be ONE with God, to be IN UNION and to know Source is within FULLY 24/7 activating through me, to me, and all around me now.

I am from Montana originally. My dad was in the Air Force for 21 years, so we traveled a lot; mostly through the northern United States and in Europe. I am a God-Lover, I love, LOVE Spirit, and the Creator, and I have been in the God-game a long time. After an encounter at an early age, I felt called to the ministry/service... I have always felt extra sensitive to things of the Spirit. At the time, that course led me to the only thing I knew to actually be in "ministry": Bible school, then graduate school seminary. Later, I founded Swiftfire International—our (God's and my) ministry.

About six years into ministry, though, I began to experience some serious dis-ease issues. By that time, I had already written books, spoken at conferences around the world, and was hosting my own television show, "Swiftfire with Sharnael Wolverton" in the USA and Canada. My dis-ease issues developed mostly because I was working 120 hours a week, traveling four days a week, and making some especially stupid choices in my "diet." My "diet," you ask? Well, it included four to six Coca-Colas a day, Ranch Doritos by the bag, and Rice Krispie bars by the box. These were basically my main food groups at the time. Suffice it to say, that did not end up working out for me very well.

Simultaneously, along with my health issues I was also going through marital issues, which led to my becoming an involuntarily-divorced-single-mom-of-three, facing poverty. I barely had money to pay the rent at times. People made donations to my family for Christmas, for school uniforms, and groceries for my kids. There were times we could barely keep the lights on. I persisted. I had to. At that time, I knew no other way.

After years of poor diet and very western, very medical, and very drug-based "health care" which only led to more side effects, I was finally introduced to another way, a natural way that led me to balance and EASE in my body. Da Da Da—SELF CARE. (Pretend that da da da sound is like the musical trumpet-type sound that introduces something cool...)

This "natural path" led me to nutrition, juicing, essential oils, Raindrop Technique®, detoxing, Keto, energy, frequency, beliefs, conscious language, understanding the Bio-Field and a lot of other things that helped me get *me* back into alignment. I was able to create balance for myself and clear some of the dis-ease issues I experienced in the past. As my body was restored on this path, several dreams from Spirit pointed me towards becoming a naturopathic doctor in order to learn more and help others as well. I believe in miracles and prayer, for sure, and I also know that choice, will, energy, beliefs, and lifestyle all play a huge role within 'whole health.' God created us. I love God. I love God-people, and I much prefer us lining up with God-choices that help us thrive in our created self.

Let's be straight up honest here: I don't care how many prophetic words you have, I don't care how many dreams you have, I don't care how many goals you have; if you're sick in bed, stuck in weird negative programs and your marriage and life and finances are in shambles, chances are you are not being your best "you." And if you don't think you have the opportunities or the provision to do what you choose, then that's what you get. Instead, how 'bout you change your mind and create a new way? I did that; I created a way for me to get my life back.

As I shifted my health along the way, the marital and financial issues upgraded miraculously too.

RE-Member… you can't pee in the pool and hope it doesn't get everywhere… energy is the same… if things are in disarray energetically in one area of your life, it touches your whole life with the same energy. Energy doesn't take a day off. Energy doesn't make exceptions if you are having a bad day. Energy is just energy… all day long. And so are laws. Read on and I'll show you how to use science, energy and these laws to your benefit.

Today, my life is pretty cool. I am Divine health, I am married to an amazing husband (my childhood sweetheart), we have 5 beautiFULL children, and we're continuing to create our miraculous life.

That wouldn't have been possible if I had sat around waiting for things to change or just "happen."

I shifted, then everything shifted.

Like I said earlier, I had to do a bit of re-verse engineering to do this, and really enjoy "quick and easy." Today's culture would call this "hacking."

One definition:
    hack[1]
        /hak/
        verb
        1. a piece of computer code providing quick solutions to a problem
        2. a strategy or technique for managing one's time or activities more efficiently

In other words, to "hack" something means to get to the shortcut, the fast and easy way, and get the job done with simplicity and fashion.

I RE-Membered how to hack my Miracles.

By the way, I say RE-Membered on purpose. Because RE- means to do again and STAY... and Membered is to be ONE with God, to be IN UNION and to know Source is within FULLY, 24/7 activating through me, to me, and all around me now. (You may see consistent weird emphasis in spelling or contractions in this book, like RE-Member and RE-Mind, JoyFULL etc, this is fully ON PURPOSE for emphasis: RE-Member because I mean this literally... RE: do again; Membered: to member or Union in Christ; to know God is inside... not separate. You will see me referring to RE-Membering and RE-Minding through this book.)

As I RE-Member Miracles and keep RE-Membering (stay in 'this', God is in me, activating through me now), I shift my world.

I have now traveled to 41 countries teaching these new truths and revelations—"hacks"—and I also use social media to ignite my world to Truth, Love and Miracles DAILY.

My mission is to empower purpose, health, and wealth. My mission is to ignite others to MIRACLES, MOMENT-TO-MOMENT. And this is also my passion. My purpose is to help you create your own desire in manifestation. The word DESIRE means "Of The Father." We all have dreams within that God has ignited in us.

The good news is we don't have to fight or stress or strive for it. When you are in a dark room, all you have to do is turn the Lights on.

God is Light; the Father of Lights and Source sent us here to BE Light and bring multiplications of Light.

I invite you to RE-Member and to KNOW… you picked up this book for a reason. This is your day.

Let me help RE-Mind you of your already installed tools within YOU.
- Maybe you are that person going through relationship issues?
- Maybe you are that person going through financial issues?
- Maybe you are that person seeing negative pattern after negative pattern… and it has been a longgggg ride of experiencing these?
- Maybe you have some health stuff going on?
- Maybe you just know there is more?

No matter what your situation is, EVERYTHING IS SHIFT-ABLE. Y-O-U are Shift-Able from the inside out. You are the only one who can affect your purpose. Y-O-U.

Let me show you how YOU can "fix" you… "HELP me HELP YOU"… (imagine Tom Cruise/Jerry McGuire voice).
- There are no coincidences.

- This is Your turn.
- This is Your Time.
- You have the same abilities I have to create your perfect, miraculous life.
- Read this book, apply it and see your TRANS-Formation now.

Let's do this!

Chapter 2

What is Frequency and the Bio-Field?

Let's start with some basics.

Everything has frequency and/or vibration. In fact, WE are electric beings. We have roughly 50 trillion living cells within us, and each cell is electric.

Our bodies are 67 MHz on a healthy adult day. We can move up and down the scale depending on many things; what we eat and drink, what we watch and hear, who we talk to, and/or about, and many other things. As we get lower than 67 MHz, it causes issues of dis-ease. When we maintain and/or raise our frequency, we stay well. (More on this throughout the book.)

Energy can take many forms.

> *"Energy is a force that takes many forms and can be manifested in many ways. Rocks have energy. Likewise, trees, plants, soil and insects have energy."*
>
> – Karol Truman

The earth has energy too. It measures 7.8 hertz.

Even scriptures refer to frequency or vibration. Here are a few regarding the creation of earth:

Genesis 1:1 "God created the heavens and the earth, and then the Spirit (Ruach, Hebrew for breath) of God vibrated over the waters."

Genesis 1:3 "And God said, "Let there be light," and there was light." NIV

Light is energy, sound, frequency, and vibration. Light is a powerFULL force. God is the Father of Lights, and we are in God's image as Light... we are God's multiplied Light. God is still "Lighting" to us, through us and in us.

And later in scriptures, Ephesians 6:12 KJV says, "...we wrestle not against flesh and blood..." That word "wrestle" actually means *to vibrate.*

Tesla once said *"If you want to find the secrets of the universe, think in terms of energy, frequency and vibration."*

What is the Bio-Field

We are frequency, and most everything has frequency. How does this affect the Bio-Field? What IS the Bio-Field?

First off... Every living thing has one, even the earth.

bi·o·field

/ˈbīō-fēld/

noun

1. subtle energy fields that permeate the living body

Some call it an aura.

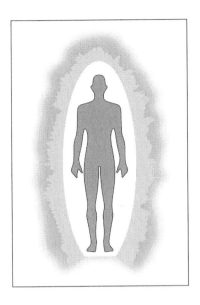

This Bio-Field is both electric and magnetic; hence, Bio. Bio means **two** or **dual**. The field is both electric and magnetic, which brings us to "electro-magnetic" field. It is a dual field, both electric—radiating out—and at the same exact time, magnetizing things TO US.

People's field average is a minimum, 10-inch radius around them, and up to 8-10 feet out in range. Dolphins have the highest frequency and the farthest range on the planet; horses come in second at around 350 feet and, of course, are way more attainable.

Our Bio-Field contains many things: code, frequency, sound, light, colors, maps, whatever. The Bio-Field, containing all the information of your immune system, as well.

And all these things mentioned above, are formed based on three things:

1. What you are thinking?
2. What you are FEELING?
3. And what you are talking about?

These things listed above create the code and/or equations within your field, radiating out and magnetizing back in. And whatever you "are," *you only get a match.*

In other words... THE LAW OF ATTRACTION.

Yep folks, it is a real thing. Science. You do not even have to believe it. It is still going happen; it is still the law. Just like gravity 'happens'... so does this.

Scientist Albert Einstein is thought to be the one credited for really identifying the law of attraction saying, "*Everything is energy, and that's all there is to it. Match the frequency of the reality you want, and you cannot help getting that reality. This is not philosophy. This is physics.*"

+Positive Electromagnetic Bio Field

This is a Positive Electromagnetic Bio-Field. Yes, I know... I am an artist for sure.

Notice the positivity in the thoughts, feeling, and speech... all sending out a beautiFULL spectrum of Love, Light, Truth, etc. All with positive equations. Also, notice how it radiates out and also magnetizes back.

-Negative Electromagnetic Bio Field

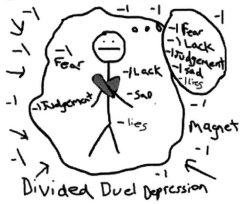

Now this is a Negative Electromagnetic Bio-Field.

Notice the negative charge associated with each word, feeling, and thought... sending out, radiating out, and only getting a match to whatever you are thinking, feeling, and talking about.

Let's break it down:

Thoughts

First, let's talk about thoughts. Our thoughts are powerFULL.

You might tell yourself that thoughts don't *matter*. But they do; thoughts literally *MATTER*. Scientists have instruments to measure the frequency and energy of your thoughts!

So many of us operate on autopilot that we do not even KNOW WHAT we are thinking. We are not consciously aware of what we are thinking and/or do not take the time to LISTEN to our own thoughts.

We run on different programs that may even have been ingrained in us since we were children or programmed into us through television, movies, videos games, parents, music and the world.

At any given moment, we are taking IN a lot of information all at once. It may be positive, negative or mixed, it may be about another person, about a particular situation, about me or about you, about how you look, how another person looks, about what your choices are, or really anything. It's ALL THE THINGS. Science says our mind thinks an average of 60,000-80,000 thoughts a day. That's almost 3,000 thoughts an hour. That's a lot to sift through.

I RE-Member I woke up one morning and heard this inner voice that said, "*What are you thinking?*" I had to actually stop myself to think about that question. What *was* I thinking? The answer is really stupid. I was actually thinking about two celebrities who were in the middle of a divorce… Sandra Bullock and Jesse James. Honestly, I was thinking about how sad I was for them both and that whole situation. I have no idea why I was thinking about this. That moment really made me wonder what else was I thinking regularly that did not contribute positively to my energy.

Suddenly, I had a mental image of this being of Light coming in and putting this plastic, white spaghetti strainer over my head… what is it called? A colander?? Attached to the plastic was a Post-it note. It just read, 'Philippians 4:8.' I had to look it up, and I encourage you to, as well. Basically, it tells you all the things that you *should* be thinking: things that are lovely, things that are pure, things that are good news, whatever is right, whatever is admirable, whatever is excellent, and praise worthy. You know, *that* kind of stuff. Think of *these* things…

I was pretty sure that was not happening very much in my own life... you know, thinking of good things; even having the discipline to think of good things.

I began monitoring my thoughts a little more and realize just how much autopilot had taken over!

Later that night I was watching the news, and I heard that question on the inside again, "*What are you thinking?*"

Again, I had to ask myself, "What *was* I thinking?" Well, I was thinking about the news and all the negative things that were coming out of that boxed screen in front of me.

Then I heard, "*Is this good news?*"

I had to be honest... "no."

I immediately got out of the bed and put Post-it notes all over my house, even in and around my 'mom van' with the question, "What are you thinking?'

This way, I would be conscious of literally every thought I was thinking, moment to moment with a little bit more discipline, and a lot more monitoring. It seemed to really help, actually.

Now my question to you is, "What are you *really* thinking?" I invite you and encourage you to slow down and ask yourself the same thing.

A similar situation happened with being awakened (while asleep) to an inner voice inside. This time I awoke to this statement, "Thoughts Matter!"

It sounded authoritative and echoed through me.

I knew that voice inside was not just saying, "yeah, like, thoughts matter... it is cool."

It was more like, "**THOUGHTS MATTER!**"

Not just, "pay attention to this big time!" ... But I knew that it meant "thoughts matter" as in physics, as in create, as in atoms, ions, and molecules.

The more I studied and looked into it, the more I found out that it is true.

Guess what? Every single thought matters, as in *manifests*. And thoughts have *frequency*. A thought can be as strong as 55 times more powerFULL than a 50-kilowatt broadcasting station sending a message around the world.

So, if we're thinking about fear, we not only send this "fear message" around the world, but way "closer to home," we send it to our bodies and into our field. Whatever we're thinking starts a chemical cascade of different things that happens inside our bodies. We create and release around 1500 negative chemicals throughout our body. This affects our physical health, especially if it is fear that we're thinking, or anything fearful in nature... When we think it in our brain, cortisol is released, among other things. This sends the body into what's known as "fight or flight" mode, which causes any of the following symptoms:

- Weight gain
- Stress
- Dehydration of skin, which causes wrinkles
- Stomach issues
- Weakened immune system
- Graying of hair

You wanna be fat, sick, and old-looking? Live in fear perception/programs.

As a man thinketh in his/her heart... so is he/she. (Proverbs 23:7)[b]

So, let's think about the good things.

When we think about good things, we have an opposing set of positive chemicals release... again around 1500 of them. These positive chemicals all create a symphony of life, love, which in turn, boosts immunity and recharges cells. This is what gives you supernatural strength and creates energetic responses as well, attracting the positive.

> James Allen was quoted saying, *"The mind is a master weaver both of the inner garment of character and the outer garment of circumstance, and that, as they may have hitherto woven in ignorance and pain they may NOW weave in enlightenment and happiness."*

In other words, we get to choose our thoughts, which create for us; our body shifts internally, and our Bio-Field externally... which then shifts our life. Choose wisely. You are creating one way or another... why not create cool stuff?

Feelings

We are electric beings, but your heart is the most electrical part of your body. Have you ever just walked in a room and FELT tension? Or like something was OFF? We feel energy and vibrations in the room through our body. We feel the Bio-Field of others. Not just with our heart but with the water in our body being an average of 75 to 90 percent water and our brain at almost 80 percent, our water actually feels the waves of the field. (again, go study the book "*The Hidden Messages in Water.*")

---

b   I am going to mention a few Bible verses in this book. Please know that as I mention these scriptures, I am coming at this from a place of quantum physics, not religion or denomination. I am a spirit being and I happen to love God; you may have your version and that is totally cool with me.

We are receivers feeling the vibes of others and the vibes of the room, even without words. We also send out our own vibrations… especially with our heart!

During my undergraduate studies, I did one of my internships in cardiac rehab. Part of my internship was to observe heart surgery a couple of times. I was always so fascinated because the surgeons would talk about the 'blue currents,' or *light*, that was within the hearts of the people receiving the operations. At the time, I shelved this information and jokingly called it the "Blue Light Special." Years later it clicked for me. Our hearts are the biggest frequency generators in our body. Our heart has frequency, it has energy, it has a current—this flicker or a flash of blue light.

That Blue Light Special IS **SPECIAL**! That current in your body shoots a message to your brain and your brain responds, depending on what you're thinking, good or bad. Your brain responds by releasing tons of bio-physiological chemicals throughout your body.

Check this out: according to Dr. Rollins McCarty at Heart Math, the electrical power of a heart signal (EKG) is up to 100,000 times stronger than the electric signal of a brain (EEG). The magnetic field of a heart is 5,000 times stronger than that of a brain. We send out more energy through the heart than the brain. The heart is our biggest energy center in our body. Your feelings, your heart, are stronger than your brain. Really take that in. Feelings are the real DEAL. Feelings CREATE.

Feelings do the same things to our brains and body regarding the chemicals affecting the cells and the same regarding the Bio-Field… again, lets choose wisely to get our highest choice match! We only get what we are…

Tesla once said, *"If your hate could be turned into electricity, it would light up the whole world."*

Words

God Spoke the world into existence. Source just said, "Let there be LIGHT." And there was Light and still is Light. That God is in you, Co-creating with you now with every word you say.

If you have never studied the science of Cymatics, check it out. And again, I also encourage you to look into "The *Hidden Messages in Water*" by Dr. Masaru Emoto. Both of these topics will give you great insight, and if you search it up on YouTube, you have a visual. It is so fascinating to me, this science thing. What we say has sound/resonance, and this sound/resonance not only has frequency, but it also *creates*.

Thoughts matter, feelings matter, and yep... our words *MATTER*.

I'm going to mention a few Bible verses here, but please know that as I mention these scriptures I am coming at this from a place of quantum physics, not religion or denomination. I am a Spirit Being and I happen to love God; you may have your version and that's totally cool with me. Your road and path are your own, but, seriously, check these out:

"By your words you will be justified, and by your words you shall be condemned." Matthew 12:37

"Speak those things that are not as though they were." Romans 4:17

"There is death and life in the power in the tongue." Proverbs 18:21

"He sent out his word and healed them..." Psalm 107:20 NIV

For, "Whoever would love life and see good days must keep their tongue from evil and their lips from deceitful speech." 1 Peter 3:10 NIV

"...speak(s) with wisdom and faithful instruction is on her tongue." Proverbs 31:26 NIV

"Set a guard over my mouth, Keep watch over my lips." Psalm 141:3

"The words of the reckless pierce like swords, but the tongue of the wise brings healing." Proverbs 12:18 NIV

These are just a few of the scriptures that talk about the power of words and language. There is an awesome book called *Conscious Language*[c] by my dear friend and co-missioner Robert Tennyson Stevens[d] that I encourage you to get on the subject that will give you even more insight.

Words direct and shape energy. When you use words, you are casting your thoughts into the Earth's magnetic force and energy field, which create reality (Good or Bad).

The COMBO in Union

Words have power. They fill our Bio-Fields with substance and matter. When words, thoughts and FEELINGS work together there is even more power. The word "LOVE" is the highest frequency word. But when the word "LOVE" is spoken in love?? With feelings of love and thoughts of love?? This is a whole new equation… literally.

Feeling love in your heart puts love in your mind, and when you speak with love and use words of love, that frequency is amplified. When we are in union with all three, thoughts/beliefs, words and feelings, we get miracles instantaneously.

Why? Because *we only get what we are*. That simple.

The Bio-Field is crucial because you radiate in code what you feel, and what you radiate you collect back magnetically. It is the law of attraction.

---

c   Book can be purchased online at www.swiftfire.org/store
d   Robert Tennyson Stevens is the founder and CEO of Mastery Systems Corporation. He is a pioneer in the influence of language, imagination, facilitation, and body language.

We have brain waves and heart waves, and then our speech. When these are in union, they are even more pronounced in both electricity and magnetic abilities, giving us a match.

Again, *we get what we are.*

Chapter 3

Beliefs and Split Energy... Energetic Purgatory

As we discussed in the last chapter, our thoughts, words, and feelings *matter*. The way you think about your life, the way you feel about your life, and the way you live your life *MATTERS*.

These thoughts and feelings shape what your life becomes. What I am sharing with you is about my life and what I have RE-Membered. That energy I'm referring to, the frequency that exists in each and every body, is a real, measurable phenomenon. What we feel and think creates a symphony of things that go through our brain and our body and in turn, affects us.

As we radiate out, we then collect and/or magnetize whatever we are thinking, talking about, or feeling. As we RE-Member, God in us... in Union. When we are Love, God is Love through us. When we LOVE, miracles happen.

When we speak of the heart, mind, and mouth, what we are really talking about is BELIEFS and or Belief systems/programs.

Let's talk about the word believe. When you sound it out, it is to "be *alive*" in something, "to embody it, to walk it out, to act as if that's the truth." And what you focus on, you make room for.

Let me say this again...

What you focus on, you make room for.

We have to be careful what we're thinking. We have to really concentrate, meaning use discipline (the word discipline comes from "disciple") in every moment, from one moment to the next.

Every moment we have, we are invited to reflect on what we're thinking about, so we can be aware of what we're talking about, and be conscious of what and how we're feeling. RE-Member as a man thinketh and as a woman thinketh, in his/her heart, so is he/she.

If we believe that "we can't make it," we get that... *"not making it"* energy. The sub-conscious takes everything literal... it does not care if you had a bad day. The law is literal, and it does not take days off... if we BE ALIVE IN:

"That's just for *those guys*," or

"Oh, I have 5 kids, so it is not going to work," or

"I don't have any money in my checking account," or

"I guess I am out of luck," or

"No one's ever gonna love me," or

"All guys are —"

Or all the things and all the excuses—cancel clear[e].
We *GET THAT...*

---

e   When I say "Cancel Clear" I am saying this after I have realized I said something that will not produce a "positive" for me energetically. Re-Member God is in me creating with me and my words. (You too) Words have power and frequency. I am canceling the energy of the words and clearing the energy behind it to keep a clear path in me and my Bio-Field thus helping the POSITIVE creation process. Instead of getting mixed or negative. This will make more sense as we go.

And do you really want *THAT*? No?

So, what in the world happens if we have thoughts about one thing but feelings about something completely different on the same subject? Huh? That can get a little interesting, right? You and I both know that this can be a pretty regular occurrence in the 60,000 thoughts per day situation (cancel clear) for us to be in limbo about a subject.

We could be really excited about something and the next second have complete fear about it. Or maybe mentally have a not-so-nice but reasonably logical idea about something, and our heart causes us to have hope for something bigger and happier about it at the same exact time. We could be feeling one thing, thinking something else and talking about something else... all in different directions... How does this look energetically, and how does this affect us in the creation process? Can this send "mixed" signals radiating out and in? In other words, split energy.

Well, here's a picture of what a Bio-Field looks like that has split energy.

James 1:6-8 But when you ask you must believe and not doubt, the one who doubts is like a wave of the sea, blown and tossed by the wind. That person should not expect from the Lord. Such a person is double minded and their loyalty is divided between God and the world.

Notice there are a lot of pluses, and there are a lot of minuses.

When we have the positives along with the negatives, we basically cancel out our creations...

Imagine: One (+1) love in your heart (+1) love in your mind, but then a (-1) saying something unloving, untrue or out of jealously or fear or judgement... We get a 1+1-1=1.

Imagine we have a bill to be paid. We have hope in our heart to RE-Member God in us is Abundance (+1) but our heart thinks about our last bad experience with money (-1). Then we call a friend and ask for a prayer with a negative spin because "money isn't here to pay this bill." Or "I don't have the money, can you please pray?" That's actually a (-1) because you are stating by fact and decree that you don't have it and the energy behind it is "accepting" and being alive in lack.

Energy says, *"IT MUST BE REALLY IMPORTANT THAT SHE DOES NOT HAVE THE MONEY BECAUSE SHE KEEPS THINKING ABOUT IT and TALKING ABOUT IT!"*

YIKES!

Hope (+1), bad experience (-1), ask for prayer in a negative way (-1)= (-1) you have a tiny hope which is positive but then a 'radiating double negative' while 'attracting the negative' equation, so you don't get your creative miracle. You stay exactly where you are.

RE-Member: energy IS literal. It does not care if you're having a bad day. What you focus on you make room for.

We can literally 1+1-1-2+1-3+1-2—all day long... this is what I call *ENERGETIC Purgatory.*

This isn't a fun place to be. And you know what? So many people do not even know they are stuck because of this. When I was stuck in this place, I had no idea I was creating this.

Before the time when I began to wake up, everything "*happened* to me." Now I *see*: I CO-CREATE my world. I am the Co-author and Co-creator of my destiny. I am the Co-captain of my ship with SOURCE.

So many people I know are there... praying to God to get them out of the situation, when in all reality, God is inside saying PLEASE LET ME OUT! Let's create COOL STUFF! Please let's make some MIRACLES TODAY, TOGETHER!

If we BE ALIVE (believe) IN TRUTH, IN OUR HEART, that we are CO-CREATORS (because we are) and we get into RE-Membering UNION IN SOURCE. It can look like this:

I am Abundance (+1)

I talk about and DECREE "I am Abundance now" (+1)

I feel in my heart and imagine FEELING the abundance flowing out of me... (+1)

1+1+1=3

> I AM Abundance +1 Heart
> I Am Abundance +1 Mind
> I Am Abundance +1 Talk
> 1+1+1=3

Now we are going somewhere!

Now I know this isn't 'real' math but knowing God is in us, and SOURCE is Abundance which is a (+1) MIND BODY AND SPIRIT that's really **ONE** to the third power.

$$1+1+1=3 \text{ actually } 1^3$$

The key is staying in alignment with all three, thoughts, feelings and words, all in the positive directions of creation. Now, think back to Matthew: "Where two or three are gathered in my name, there I Am." When we have the alignment of the mind, heart, mouth, and speech, that's where magic happens. That's where **Miracles** happens.

RE-Member your PERFECT alignment NOW!

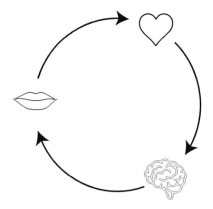

Chapter 4

The Earth Energy Field

The earth also has a measurable frequency or standard equation. It is also sometimes called the unified field. In 1952, a man named Winfried Otto Schumann discovered the resonance and/or electric field of the earth. There are electric currents or electromagnetic waves that actually band around like an electric belt around the earth. The average is about 7.83 Hertz. We are all interconnected in this electric belt around the earth, and we are affected *by it* and at the same time we are *affecting it*.

Hear the Truth. We are all connected.
Separation is an illusion.

When different significant global changes happen in and on the Earth, it has affected the frequency of the earth and those who inhabit it. For example, when the OJ Simpson situation happened, the frequency of the earth all resonated at a higher vibration. Other events in the past where this occurred include Princess Diana's wedding, Princess Diana's funeral, 9/11 and more. All these times and significant global events, because of social media and the combination of the media, combine our thoughts, our words, and our mindsets on a single focal point increasing the tension and the stress causing an energy shift on the planet... all measureable on instruments!

Not only can the earth's electric belt change significantly because of the people who inhabit it, but it also can be changed by external forces like solar flares, full moons, retrogrades in the galaxies, or other issues in the heavens or cosmos.

What we're thinking or feeling can actually be a direct effect of what's going on externally and the electric belt or "current" of the earth and all of those who inhabit it.

When external things happen, it can cause dreams, visions, ideas, renewed creativity, irritability, mood swings, over-hunger (or hunger for weird stuff), flu symptoms, fatigue, energy, anxiety, restless sleep, loss of appetite, increased appetite, hot flashes, surges of energy, vertigo, blurred vision, …it affects everyone differently because we are all different.

The best way to maintain harmony within and STAY in THE Union Field is doing things like:

Grounding	Exercise
Drinking water	Fasting
Rest as required	Sunshine
Eat high-vibe food	Nature
Essential Oils	Music
Crystals	Art
Sauna	Meditation
Foot baths	Raindrop
Epsom salt baths	Massage
EMFs (Electromagnetic Frequency shields)	

The good news is these jolts can help bring us to our better selves with better behaviors too. It gives us the opportunity to clear the DNA, which is critical in the creation process (we will talk about this more in chapter 12-13). If we recognize what's happening and understand that we are not crazy, this gives us the opportunity to SEE what's showing up on the surface. We can touch it all with love and transmute it… to a new sound of LOVE. This also changes everything.

LOVE is THE STABALIZER.
LOVE is THE PLUMBLINE.

As negative patterns surface, things that may have been suppressed/depressed/trapped deep inside from long ago (we may not even have known they existed) and then as we REALize, we can transmute them by "feeling the hell outta them!" Literally! Bringing us to a new upgrade AND a smoother miracle creation process.

Chapter 5

The Collective Consciousness

In the last chapter, I discussed the effects of a collective consciousness and how it affected the earth and how the earth was actually affected by our beliefs, thoughts, and feelings.

Sometimes our thoughts, feelings and our beliefs—our programs—are not exactly our own. If we are not careful, we can take on external programs from the unified earth field on a collective level.

"If we try to pick out anything by itself, we find it hitched to everything else in the universe."

– John Muir

The environment of our upbringing can program us, too. We can be programmed through television, through people around us, through well-meaning friends and family, through movies, through billboards, mobile devices, computers, newspapers, social media; we're absorbing information 24 hours a day in multiple ways.

Science says we take in 400 billion bits of information per second. We are calculating things we don't even realize we are calculating. We are taking in and processing things like gravity, temperature, body function management, surroundings etc. moment-to-moment. The human brain is loaded daily with 34GB of information. People receive about 100 to 5000 words (or 23 words per second) in a half a day during *waking hours.*

American psychiatrist Edward Hallowell commented, *"Never in human history have our brains had to work so much information. As of today, we now have a generation of people who spend many hours in front of the computer monitor or a cell phone who are so busy processing the information received from all directions."*

How much of this do we "take on?" Honestly, this has to make a difference in our choices, doesn't it? I mean it has to make a difference in what we're feeling too, right? How much of this information is all about the POSITIVE (+1s)? Think about a negative person like Debbie Downer. Imagine how much of this is the negative (-1)?

With social media, we can spread good or bad vibes across the world with the click of a finger. Whether it is true or not, it's out there. I mean, we've all heard the thing about fake news. So many things that are published are absolutely not true and once they're out there and for all of us to see, talk about, and come into agreement with, then it is too late and most of the time they don't go back and fix it. If they do, it is on the back page of another edition, but it isn't in the headlines, is it?

How does this affect our co-creations and our co-missions?

Let's do some math and look at the equations regarding social media alone.

Let's say you're on Facebook and you have 1500 "friends." Now we'll say, each of your 1500 friends have a minimum of 400 friends each. You make a post about what a crappy day you're having and all the reasons why everyone should hate their life because of the economy or politics or ... (insert gripe here). Well now you're 1500 friends may have seen that post and then it shows up in their feed of 400 people each. Multiply that by 1500 and that gives your crappy day a chance to go out to 600,000 people sending a vibration of negativity.

This doesn't even consider the times when they comment back... giving it energy, sharing it, giving it energy or giving it a "like," which also amplifies energy.

Now, they have physically and energetically laid their eyes on it. They have probably read it, or maybe talked about it amongst their friends, asked questions about it, wondered what in the world is going on with you, wondering what can they do; they get into chatty gossip, and the negativity spirals. Blah, blah, energetic BLAH.

Even if only half of them talk about it... that's still -300,000 in the negative. If they're emotional about it (the add a negative heart equation), obviously they're thinking about it because they just put their eyes on it, so that multiplies. $3 \times -300,000$ gives you a whopping -900,000 in the negative. Good job creating.

Earlier I mentioned "negative prayer". Let me explain.

Let's say somebody that you know and love very much is really sick and in the hospital. You take a picture of them with their IV's and tubes coming out all kinds of places... now you post that on Facebook under the umbrella of "prayer."

That picture then gets passed around, shared, and tagged, and now everybody is talking about "Johnny" who is super sick and probably will not make it, how it happened, and how terrible it is, and what about his kids, and what about his job, and will he ever survive? They get their heart in it, they get their mind in it, and they've all connected visually to the stupid picture that you posted of your suffering friend that's now gone viral.

Even if only one-third of everybody saw it, talked about it, and had their heart in it, you're still talking about hundreds of thousands in the negative. All that energy is not only coming back to you but also going towards the person that you posted about.

Now imagine they're holding that image and they're holding that person *in that image, TO that image* of staying sick because that's the last thing "on the screen" of their minds... and computers or phones... in code.

Group Texts

What about group texts? Have you ever been held hostage in a group text or a group thread? If positive, this can be amazing but if it is negative, holy cow! Not our highest choice.

Ugh.

So, what can we do about it? How can we make a shift so we're spreading positivity and set up all the negatives literally? How do we change the equation? How do we create something beautiFULL and miraculous?

What if we posted a beautiFULL picture of our friend in the highest vitality with a warm message merely stating, "Please vote victory for my dear friend Johnny and see him in his THRIVING divine health now!"

Then everybody would hold *that* image, and everyone would hold *that* vison as the message spreads.

**See, the word imagination broken down just means to
*"image—a—nation."***

We have the power to choose our images, to choose our words, to choose our feelings and post accordingly in our highest choice. Social media and the news and all media could actually be used to our benefit.

It makes you wonder at times what exactly is behind the agenda of most of the programs on television. There's a reason why it is called programming, y'all.

Most of all, media has programs of division: whether it is race, gender, or politics. Look at the commercials: telling you what health issues you *have* and telling you how to use all the "normal" medications or pharmakeia to get "better." (The word "pharmakia" by definition means "witchcraft". Look it up.

Almost every television show in this age "IMAGES" women and children abused or in a less-than state, and there's always that one person in every television show that has cancer and is going to suffer and die. <CANCEL CLEAR NOW>

We have to come above it. I invite you to rise above that and to turn off anything that would program US in the negative. Stay clear of even watching or liking or participating in anything negative.

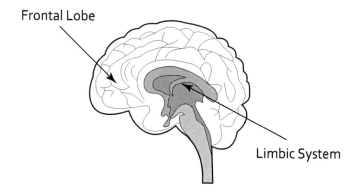

Frontal Lobe

Limbic System

Your limbic system cannot tell the difference between what is really happening on a screen as being real, or what's happening in your living room as being real. Everything that you can imagine matters, everything that you can imagine affects your body, everything that you put your eyes on, your limbic system associates it with it actually happening.

So be awake and stay AWAKE NOW so your MIRACLE MAKING is ABUNDANT!!

Chapter 6

The Science of Judgment and Forgiveness

"Opinions are like witchcraft." Bob Jones[f], a dear mentor and spiritual father to me would always say that.

o·pin·ion

> /əˈpinyəns/
>
> *noun*
>
> 1. a judgment given without real experience or first hand knowledge.

judg·ment

> /ˈjəjmənt/
>
> *noun*
>
> 1. to decide something as fact with or **without** evidence or experience to support it

None of us have all the information to ever be able to make an informed judgment.

A lot of times, people will say things flippantly or even choose to make a decision or a judgment about something or someone without really having all the full knowledge of everything that is surrounding it, and we have to be really, really careful doing this!

---

f   Bob Jones (1930-2014) was a prophetic seer who moved with a clear revelatory gifting accompanied by the gifts of healing and miracles.

Scripture even says to touch not God's anointed (I Samuel 26). When we 'touch God's anointed,' it actually means touch Gods men and women. When we "touch" the DNA of anyone in God's image, scripture says 'touch not the God in my sons,' (those who are in God's image).

This is with an understanding that not everyone knows God, believes in God, or has any relationship in this loving awakening. I am saying regardless of anyone's choice in beliefs, we are still in the image of Source and carry God-DNA, and we are not supposed to touch God's people.

There are repercussions and consequences that we will discuss here, not just on an electric field transaction, but on a physical, too.

First, let's talk about the electronic consequences.

We discussed that we all had a Bio-Field and an energetic field or belt all around us. Even the earth has this electronic field which I will refer to as a 'unified field.' When we make a judgment about something or someone, it is a coded transaction that goes out into, not just through your whole body, but to the Bio-Field.

Scripture says, 'judge and you will be judged.' As a matter of fact, in Matthew 7:2 it says, "For the same way you judge others you will be judged and with the measure you use it, it would be measured unto you."

> Luke 6:37 says, "Do not judge, and you will not be judged. Do not condemn, and you will not be condemned. Forgive, and you will be forgiven." NIV

Why is this?

Not only is judgment very low frequency, but if you release judgment in your own Bio-Field, RE-Member, you can only get a match. So basically, you're putting a target on yourself to be judged.

Judgment carries a frequency signal. That signal will go out and radiate and it will magnetize that judgment signal right back to you; **again *you*** *only get a match.* This is an electronic transaction that's released into your Bio-Field that comes back to you.

Let's talk about the physical consequences. Not only do you have physical consequences because of the karma that is produced in judging others and allowing that to come back, but there is also a physical affect in your limbic system. In the last chapter we discussed the limbic system. The limbic system is that part of your brain behind the frontal lobe that is the seat of all emotions. AND, the limbic system cannot tell the difference between what's real and what isn't. It cannot tell the difference between you or me.

In other words, if you're judging someone else your brain releases chemicals throughout your body as if *you yourself* are being judged. You judge someone else, but your body registers it as if it is YOUR experience; both the pain and the consequence of that judgment. It is literally as if *you are judging you* because we're in a unified field and because we're **all made** in the image of God. And as Bono of U2 would say, *"There is no them only us."*

> Galatians 6:7 "Do not be deceived, God is not mocked; for whatever a man sows, this he will also reap." NASB
>
> Romans 12:5 says, "so in Christ we, though many, form one body, and each member belongs to all the others." NIV

1 Corinthians 12:12-27 ESV:

> For just as the body is one and has many members, and all the members of the body, though many, are one body, so it is with Christ. For in one Spirit we were all baptized into one body— Jews or Greeks, slaves or free—and all were made to drink of one Spirit. For the body does not consist of one member but of many. If the foot should say, "Because I am not a hand, I do not belong to the body," that would not make it any less a part of the body. And if the ear should say, "Because I am not an

eye, I do not belong to the body," that would not make it any less a part of the body. If the whole body were an eye, where would be the sense of hearing? If the whole body were an ear, where would be the sense of smell? But as it is, God arranged the members in the body, each one of them, as he chose. If all were a single member, where would the body be? As it is, there are many parts, yet one body. The eye cannot say to the hand, "I have no need of you," nor again the head to the feet, "I have no need of you." On the contrary, the parts of the body that seem to be weaker are indispensable, and on those parts of the body that we think less honorable we bestow the greater honor, and our unpresentable parts are treated with greater modesty, which our more presentable parts do not require. But God has so composed the body, giving greater honor to the part that lacked it, that there may be no division in the body, but that the members may have the same care for one another. If one member suffers, all suffer together; if one member is honored, all rejoice together. **Now you are the body of Christ and individually members of it.**

God knew this. God created the whole thing—the laws. That's why he's given us so many different opportunities to RE-Member staying in all the names of God and especially LOVE!

Jesus himself, who many wrote about, is all God and all man. He understood these laws. He understood the science and the code. He understood the body. So much so, that even while He is nailed to the cross, he's actually making sure that he himself does not have any judgment or unforgiveness towards the people that are doing these terrible things to him.

He calls out to God on the cross and says, "Forgive them for they know not what they do." He's actually crying out to God to ask for forgiveness for the people who are doing these terrible things, as they were dividing up his mantle right before him.

Get this, in Luke 23:34, look up the Strong's Concordance: if you breakdown the word "forgive," it is G863, and that word forgive? … Get ready… it is not necessarily a ***word that spoken*** but it is a *cry*. It is a *sound,* and thus, *vibration*. It is a sound of remitting. That word "remitting?" Are you ready? The remitting means ***to cancel, to clear!***

Right there in that moment, with a sound to the Father and to all, He is asking God to cancel clear the vibration of what these people are doing "for they know not what they do."

> G492—they "know." That word "know" means their "perception, their experience, their judgment, their opinion…" (which can be like witchcraft) not what they do.

That word "do," is G4160 which means, "to produce, to author, to manifest, to create."

Jesus is asking God to remit, or *cancel,* the sound of the code within these men and their Bio-Field. These men who are doing awful things to Him, yet Jesus is still saying, "Will you please cancel clear whatever is going on with them, with these people right now, as they're doing these terrible things because they don't even have a clue what vibration and karma code they are creating and producing and sending out ***to get their own match…***"

Now that we have discussed the ramifications of judgment not only an electronic transaction but on a physical level, I hope that you understand and can be more aware and awake to any judgments that you may be making.

As I awoke to this, I was absolutely appalled by all of the random judgments that I had made while on autopilot. The more and more in tune I became, the more I realized how subtle judgment can be.

I'll give you a couple embarrassing (but true) examples.

My husband and I were driving to a city that we had never been to before. I do not like being late because my word is my bond. Anyone who knows me knows that, if for whatever reason I am running late then I will contact the person immediately and let them know what's going on and the correct time that I'll be there.

Normally, I leave way early so I'll get to my destination early. I'd rather be there earlier than late just because my word is my word, and I like to keep my energies straight. Well, in this particular situation, we did not leave early and we were in a city that we've never been in. We were very unfamiliar with it, and the GPS in our car was taking us all the wrong ways.

This was making us even more late. Which was stressing me out. I contacted the people and let them know we're going to be late, which really bugged me. And as the GPS was saying, "turn on so and so street." We noticed over and over that there weren't a whole lot of street signs anywhere to even look at to gauge where we were or where we were going.

I RE-Member making a comment to Brian. I said, "You would think this city would have actual signs so we would know where to go!"

As soon as I said it, I realized what I did, and I cancel-cleared.

I mean, basically, what I was saying is, if I was in charge I would do it better!

All ego. Super uncool.

This of course is coming from a person who exemplifies the very definition of one who has never been in any position of governing a city and still thinking that I knew how to do it better.

Maybe there was a storm a week before and all the signs came down, who knows? Maybe it was not in their budget to get a second group of signs after the storm?

I personally don't know why. I am obviously making all these scenarios up. The point is, I am just saying that I have never governed a city so who am I to think I could do it better? And yet, here I spouted out some very judgmental not-so-cool statement that I had to cancel-clear.

I'll give you one more example to really bring it home.

During the presidential campaign, there was a certain candidate that was supposed to be giving their support to another presidential candidate that was selected for the nomination. When it came time for this person who was nominated, to accept their nomination, there were all kinds of folks out there who were supposed to be contributing with their support. One in particular did not.

A lot of people were upset. As a matter of fact, it was all over Facebook the next day. People were expressing their disappointment for this person's lack of follow-through on his commitment. I almost posted something myself. But, it was right after I had gotten the whole "-1 + 300 x mind, heart, words equation" so I did not end up posting.

I noticed a friend of mine had posted regarding his disappointment. I almost commented about three or four different times and then wisely erased it with surety. Then finally I just did something that was really very simple. I merely hit "like." 'Like" meaning I agreed with this person's disappointment with the guy who did not support the candidate who was chosen, even though at one time he agreed to do that.

Simultaneously, I didn't really think of it for a little bit, but I received a message that some lady was mad at me for charging for a conference that we were hosting.

The conference that we were organizing was going to cost a minimum $35,000. We were only charging $45.00 a person. The $35,000 covered rent for the building, payment for the guest speakers, transportation costs for the speakers, lodging for the speakers, and food costs. There are a lot of expenses that are involved when you're hosting a big conference like that. We had been doing it for 20 years. The $45.00 per person is just to help pay for some of it and usually does not even cover it most of the time. It is just an investment for those participating to come help support the cost a bit.

Anyway, someone was upset about this conference charge and had posted it all over Facebook. It happened to be a spiritual conference and this person happened to be religious (no judgment), and she was saying all these things like, "Well, the last time I looked, the Bible was free and ministry should be free so Dr. Sharnael shouldn't be charging for the conference." All over my personal Facebook page and hers.

Immediately, I was thinking, *what in the world is this lady doing?* She has no idea what it takes to do a $35,000 conference. At that time, I had been doing conferences this size and bigger for 17 years. Honestly, in reality, she had probably never even hosted a backyard barbeque for four let alone a $35,000 budget conference. (No judgment) This lady just **did not know**... she had *no experience* in this...

I was so upset. 😔

I commented to explain that someone had to pay for all of the expenses and that's just how conferences work.

When I walked out of my office I happened to walk through the living room when I noticed the politician I had just judged on Facebook with my "like," who was on the news explaining there were a lot of reasons *why* he did what he did, and then commented about how he had been doing this for *17 years*!!!!

It stopped me in my tracks.

Sound familiar?

I instantly saw the connection. The sowing and reaping was almost immediate. Even the same platform was used for judgment in this case

Facebook. I had judged someone who had 17 years' experience in something that I didn't have any understanding about and someone now judged me on my own 17 years.

I had merely judged, just with a simple "like" on Facebook, and within minutes I am being judged myself publicly. What the Heck!?

Yeah, this stuff is really serious. Laws are laws. It's not just scriptures. It's universal law.

Drop a pen from a level position. It falls to the ground because of gravity. This is also universal law, just like the law 'when we judge we get judged.' Let's keep our energy clear and only sow love. Let's be way more aware and attentive to what our thoughts are, to what our heart feels, to what our mouth is saying and even to the work we do by the click of our mouse.

With the social media aspect, this is especially dangerous. I find in my experience, people are more prone to say things on social media that they wouldn't normally say to someone's face... because the human aspect is perceived as 'removed.' It's all too easy now to armchair-quarterback a situation from your comfortable couch with a laptop to top it off, actually thinking there are no ramifications. Let me tell you... THERE STILL ARE! *You* may not be connecting them, but it is a law.

And as I spoke in the previous chapters on 'collective consciousness,' when we judge in public while getting others to join us, it is massive "judge energy" OUT and "judge energy " karma BACK! Yikes!

If we put something out there with a low frequency, for others to join us in that "campaign" or "transaction," well, now the equation has amplified and joined force. Good or bad.

RE-Member to the **MEASURE WE** judge, it comes back to us. So, judge public... get a public judgment back!

This doesn't even take into account that some judgements may actually be based on *incorrect* info. Maybe we are misinformed, or we don't have enough information... so half-truths are dealt out and they spread. It takes so much more to undo all of that has been spread, even when TRUTH is eventually presented.

This illustrates the fake news situation. (A whole other topic)

Whatever You Give Ear To

So, what do we do when someone gives us a call to tell us something, regardless of whether it is judgmental, true/false, or worse... twisted truth?

> Mark 4:24 says, "Take heed to what you hear. With the same measure you use it, it will be measured unto you; and to you who hear, more will be given."

In other words, be careful what you give your ear to because if you listen to gossip or judgment, then energetically you are still in the equation and you're still in the transaction!

It will be measured unto you, and *more* will be given.

Good or bad.

Anyone who knows me knows if they send me anything in text, social media, any kind of judgments or whatever, my response is something similar to this, "I love you. Please never send me anything like this again." And then I usually send them my video on YouTube explaining the power of collective consciousness and judgment.

If they call me with negative information about someone, my response is usually something like this, "I love you. I am sad you're sad. How about we get on a 3-way call and talk to the person directly and get this worked out together. I'd rather you talk to them than to me."

Keeps my energy clear.

God so Loved the World

We are to love… and to love everyone without judgment. No matter, religion, gender, choices etc. RE-Member, separation is an illusion. When we love others, we are really loving ourselves. The scripture says God so loved the world. It does not say God so loved the *church*. I am sure God loves the church, but God loves the *world* and we are supposed to be in God's image loving everyone as well. We are not of this world but being in this world… PRE-sent as a present.

I foster kittens, and when we get a litter, I'll ask my youngest daughter, "Which one's your favorite?" Every. Single. Time. She responds with aggravation, "Mom you cannot do that. Isn't it fair there *are no favorites*!! Everyone is the favorite!"

We have to see *everyone as our favorites*. This includes ourselves; we have to love ourselves well.

Maybe your issue isn't judging others, but maybe it is judging yourself.

Hmmmm.

I invite you to love yourself well and to RE-Member love and to RE-Member forgiveness.

If you are judging yourself, you're releasing *that* into your body, and you're releasing that into your Bio-Field. Then you actually collect *more* judgment from others. Because RE-Member, there is *no them it is only us*.

We actually *use people* to judge us because we already feel that way about ourselves (cancel clear).

Robert Tennyson would say, *"Other people will only submit to your lowest illusion."*

So, if you judge you or hate you… you invite others to submit to this sound and then participate.

Only awakened people will see you with God eyes. Anyone else will only submit to your lowest frequency. Everything and everyone is a mirror.

We have to look at this from all avenues; not just RE-Membering to be aware of not judging others, but judging ourselves too.

The good news is, when we sow forgiveness and grace we release that into our Bio-Field to get a match. When we release forgiveness and grace, our brain registers that as forgiveness and grace to ourselves.

There is a literal sound and a frequency to 'judgment of opinions' and to 'grace and love.' There is a code to this that we emit and radiate out, which we then send throughout our body...

Let's RE-Member LOVE and RE-Mind LOVE now... and sow with wisdom.

Chapter 7

The Science of Giving

OK, fasten your seatbelts for this chapter. You're really gonna love it!

Let's talk about the science of giving!

Earlier in this book, we discussed the limbic system. The limbic system is the librarian of your whole body. It helps defragment your emotions and is actually the seat of your emotions.

I have mentioned before how your brain cannot tell the difference between something that is really happening on TV or any type of device verses REAL life. Even though you see it on television instead of actually experiencing it, your limbic system cannot differentiate between fact or fiction.

The limbic system also cannot tell the difference in time. That's why a lot of times when we do therapy or we keep talking about how we did not make cheerleader in the fourth grade, if that's really an issue, then your body can experience all the rejection and fear as if it is happening now instead of 20 years ago.

This isn't good for yourself, your body or your Bio-Field.

We spoke about how the limbic system also cannot tell the difference between you and me. So, if we judge others... we judge ourselves. It is also, not good for the cells or the Bio-Field because we just get a match back. It does not draw the line of separation between something that's happened to me versus something that's happened to you.

This is why we can hear about someone going through something awful, yet, we feel the pain and/or experience ourselves. On a positive note, if someone is going through something joyful and amazing, we also feel the same joy and amazement.

So, what about giving? Regarding giving: science proves that every time we give something, our body and our limbic system will process it as if you were giving it to **yourself FIRST!**

It stimulates the entire brain and activity in your cells to show that you were actually giving to yourself, so you have a response in your cells and in your entire body that shows you gave it to *you*. There's no line of separation that you actually gave it to someone else!

Let's look at some scriptures.

> Luke 6:38 says, "Give and it will be given unto you, in good measure, pressed down, shaken together, running over into your lap."

> The word lap means "bosom" and is G2859 in the Strong's, which means: an intimate position, a union, and intimacy.

When we give, we're giving to ourselves. There is a physical, scientific response in the body that does not know the difference between giving and receiving.

Um... RE-Member the whole thing about reaping and sowing?

> Let's look at Proverbs 11:25 NIV, "A generous person will prosper; [prosper could mean a lot of different things not just money] whoever refreshes others will be refreshed."

Hmmmm... kinda sounds like the science of the limbic system receiving, being encouraged and/or refreshed, as you give to someone else.

How about Proverbs 18:16. It says, "A man's gift makes room for him and opens the way to the presence of the great!"

OK, that word "opens" is H7337 which means: to be or grow already enlarged to make room for.

As we give, we're already positioning ourselves for enlargement.

It already comes back to us at the same time.

Deuteronomy 8:18 it says, "He's given us the *ability* to *create wealth.*"

Again, this is a chain reaction type of creation. When we give, we are charging our limbic system to do its thing... AND charging our Bio-Field to **BE** the CODE OF GIVING AND THE CODE OF GENEROSITY... which brings us a MATCH!

In Acts 20:35 NIV the bible quotes Jesus as saying, "... 'It is more blessed to give than to receive!'"

Giving shouldn't be something you do when you *can.* Giving should be a *state of mind* and a *practice.*

That word "blessed"... you know what that word *bless* means? It is *makarios* which is the Strong's G3107, and it means: to be "in a position of favor to be in a position of receiving, to be where God extends his benefits." Jesus' words say everything, "I have shown you in your physical body including down to the cells, your body is showing that when you give, you're giving to yourself."

I really like this. What does that mean as far as the Bio-Field? RE-Member "whatever we think upon so are we." So, whether you're thinking positive things are negative things, "As a man thinks in his heart so is he." Yes! If you are giving, whether it is good or bad, whatever you give will be given the same measure unto you. If you're giving money or gifts, our body translates this as a transaction to you! Then you get a match to that.

It could be instantly and/or eventually, but what you sow you reap.

Even when we pay bills or send money for a service we should send to the heart of God with love and gratitude.

What about other types of giving?

If you give criticism or judgment to "someone," your body and Bio-Field register this transaction as criticism to YOU. Your brain experiences judgment or criticism in that moment. And then it goes through all your cells as if you were being judged yourself. It goes into your Bio-Field. There's code and mapping in the Bio-Field of judgment, and then guess what? You only get a match.

So, someone will judge you back even after you judge yourself.

So, let's be super careful what we are thinking and doing!

When you catch yourself starting to judge, stop right there and replace the thoughts with gratitude. We can replace those thoughts.

Think of it like this: You're at the top of a hill and there is a car there right on the edge. You're in front of that car. If the car is a stick manual and about to roll down the hill, if you can catch it right at the top of the hill before it gets momentum, you can probably stop it with the strength of your body. AND if the car has started to roll halfway down the hill already, the momentum of that car will probably run you over (cancel clear). We have to stop thoughts in their tracks at the very start as soon as we catch it, and we have to practice this training.

> Again, "We demolish arguments and every pretension (or imagination) that sets itself up against the knowledge of our God, and we take captive *every* thought and we make it obedient." (2 Corinthians 10:5 NIV)

How do we make it obedient? We replace it! So, the instant you catch yourself, first CANCEL CLEAR, then quickly bless, and send love and light to "whomever" (which is really you!), you quickly also receive this. You give out *and* you're actually receiving first on a physical level, then on a Bio-Field level and a spiritual level.

As we practice this over and over, we can actually hardwire new paths in our brain to automatically think positive, loving thoughts. This is called *neuroplasticity*.

When we have old programming that may have trained our minds to be critical or in fear, as we practice new thoughts… we can scientifically alter our minds to go on autopilot with new thoughts and paths.

RE-Member the colander with the sticky note? "Think on THESE things?" As we are disciplined with practice, we can shift things internally. When we shift within, we also shift our Bio-Field externally which gives us a new match outcome.

Take time to practice now.

Chapter 8

Signature DNA Code

This is a really short chapter but an important one. We indeed have a lot of external issues, but let's talk about some internal issues—our genetics. We can be programmed genetically from our ancestors. All of us have DNA, and that DNA comes from our ancestors. And that DNA can have programs already installed from our ancestors. Our DNA, which resides in our body *also* has an electric field that broadcasts out into our Bio-Field. This creates your own specific energetic signature code.

This is like an energetic thumbprint… unique to only you. This, too, can cause mixed energy, if we're not careful.

For example, maybe your grandparents witnessed poverty at a very young age. (The first 6 years of life children are like sponges physically, mentally, spiritually and energetically.) Children absorb *everything* effortlessly in large amounts. This is often referred to as the 'absorbent mind.' Children develop 85% of their core brain structure by the time they are 5 years old. This affects the core foundation of the rest of their life.

Maybe because of that poverty those belief programs were formed and came into existence, and this was passed down to you genetically on a DNA level. Not only can we take on programs unconsciously, especially at our younger ages, but there is a sound or a code in a frequency that syncs with our equations and radiates out through our Bio-Field and attacks a match.

The great news is, we can change it. We can BE in agreement with Source, inside and out. We can RE-Program and RE-Member and RE-Mind now!

This is just another reason why it is absolutely crucial and important to RE-Member and RE-Mind.

Our alignment with our thoughts, feelings, and words cannot be about anything having to do with our upbringing. It cannot be about anything we are receiving externally. It cannot even be anything about what happened to our great-great-great-great-great-granddaddy. It cannot even be anything we have made up… or even anything we "see" in our current reality.

We have to STAY in Union with Truth and who Truth is and how Truth resides in you and THROUGH you.

There can be only one Truth.

Our true belief mixes with these DNA genetics and creates a unique signature code to you. More in future chapters to help you know better how to deal with DNA issues in order to have a better outcome.

Chapter 9

The DNA Phantom Affect

Before we get into more about creating, I want to lay a little bit of foundation about how important DNA and beliefs really are.

I'll just say this: thoughts become things. You have heard me say it in my videos and my teachings, now you can see it on paper. Thoughts become things: that's *matter*.

According to the Russian Academy of Sciences paper that appeared in the United States in 1995 there was a series of experiments suggesting that human DNA is directly affected by the physical world through what they believe and through DNA.

Two Russian scientists took a test tube and decided to impart quantum stuff that our world is made of and inserted it into the tube. The container was empty and even the air was taken out, but the scientists knew something was inside... photons. Using certain equipment, they could actually detect the particles inside and, of course, the light particles scattered everywhere clinging to the side of the glass clustering around the container jumping around completely energetic and orderly. They were everywhere which was precisely what was expected. Then, someone got the bright idea that they were going to inject human DNA in the tube with the photons. They wanted to see if the photons would have any effect on the influence of the DNA. It really surprised them because as they injected the DNA, the photons immediately took the structure of the DNA that was injected into the tube. It was like there was a residual force for making them bond with the DNA.

The DNA was clearly having an effect on the photons.

The next part of the experiment they decided to remove the DNA out of the tube to see what would happen to the photons without the DNA. What happened is astonishing. Even though the DNA was removed, the photons stayed in the structure of how they were once formed by the DNA even though the DNA was no longer in the tube. They called it the DNA Phantom effect similar to an experiment called the Matrix that Max Planck had identified more than 50 years earlier.

Clearly, this shows that there is a direct relationship between DNA and the energy of our world. Cells and DNA have a direct influence of matter through this form of energy.

When I think about this, I think about the Bio-Field, and I think about our ability to stay in union with the truth of who God is and what God is, in us and through us. I think about our Bio-Field or the dome around us. I think about things like Peter and his shadow. In scriptures, Peter would just walk by someone and anyone who even came into contact with his shadow was instantly healed. This was his Bio-Field. He not only understood healing, but he knew The Healer and had the belief that he, with God, could heal, and that resonated throughout his body and into his Bio-Field touching everyone and shaping everyone who came in contact with him. This affected their Bio-Field which affected their body, which brought their healing.

What does this mean to us now? This means you could walk around, drive around, be wherever you are: the post office, your school, your work, and if you RE-Member and RE-Mind that God is in you... full healing. God is the healer in you that goes into your Bio-Field and you touch others and long after your gone, you still leave a trail, a code, a DNA residue of healing in their path to touch them.

Your beliefs not only change you and your body, but your beliefs can change your world and touch your world!

This is absolutely, freaking insane-awesome.

I think about how biblically they prayed over handkerchiefs and not only left DNA on the handkerchief, but the belief system of prayer and good vibrations on the actual physical object which was transferable and freely given to someone. And even though the giver was not anywhere nearby anymore, the frequency, the DNA, and the photons in the shape of the structure of those already healed were on the handkerchief and transferable not only to the Bio-Code and the Bio-Field, but also to the person which brought miracles and healing.

Again, this is freaking awesome.

This is how powerFULL we are. This is how powerFULL you are.

Chapter 10

The Power of Replacing

Right now, think about the Statue of Liberty in your mind's eye... now, quickly think about the Eiffel Tower. That's how fast we can IMAGINE and shift energy.

All by conscious choice.

We may *make or think it's hard*, but it is not hard... it is merely a choice. Miracles are a choice.

On the flip side... as I said earlier, energy and your subconscious don't care if you're having a bad day. If your focus is on what you don't have or what you DON'T "wanna" think about, you'll create that just as easy.

Everyone now—DON'T THINK about pink elephants... See? Now you're thinking about pink elephants, aren't you?

> Philippines 4:8 AMP "Finally believers, whatever is true, whatever is honorable and worthy of respect, whatever is right and confirmed by God's word, whatever is pure and wholesome, whatever is lovely and brings peace, whatever is admirable and of good repute; if there is any excellence, if there is anything worthy of praise, think **continually** on these things (center your mind on them and plant them in your heart)."

> 1 Corinthians 2:16 AMP "But we have the mind of Christ (to be guided by God's thoughts and purposes)."

Colossians 3:2 "*Set your mind* and keep focused *habitually* on the things above (the heavenly things) not on the things on the earth…"

Why do you think there are so many scriptures having to do with having the mindset of Christ?

To set your mind are the words in one translation, *to FIX your mind* in another… takes effort… takes discipline.

Maybe God made such an effort to tell us these things because God knew that with the external, the genetic signature code and all the other things in the equation that we truly would have to be disciplined and use our mind and our hearts to stay in union: RE-Membering and RE-Minding.

My absolute favorite scripture:

2 Corinthians 10:5 NIV "We demolish arguments and every pretension (or imagination) that sets itself up against the knowledge of God (Truth) and we take captive every thought and we make it obedient to Christ."

How do we make it obedient? By replacing it.

I am reminded of a story I once heard about the Stanford marshmallow experiment with these kids and marshmallows. The kids were taken into a room one by one, privately, with a plate of three marshmallows on it. They were told that they had to sit and wait in this room until an adult came back, and to not eat the marshmallows. They were told that if they patiently waited until the adult came back that when they came back they can not only have those three marshmallows, but several more. They're not told how long the adults would be gone. The room inside only contained a table, a chair, and a plate of three marshmallows.

Some of the kids sat at the table staring at the marshmallows on the plate, and within minutes they took a bite or ate the whole plate of marshmallows. Some actually waited a little bit longer. Then they sniffed a marshmallow, picked it up, played with it and finally, some ate the marshmallows. And then there was this other thing that happened.

Some of the kids started out looking at the marshmallows but then decided it was not in their best interest to stare at the marshmallows all day. They got up, walked around, played with their tennis shoes, played with their shoelaces, played with their hair, sang songs, faced the wall, got underneath the table, or went to the corner and stared at the wall. They did whatever it took to not even look at the marshmallows. The marshmallows didn't even exist in their world. They weren't even in their vision and before you know it, the adults came back and there was the kid with their plate, marshmallows uneaten.

These kids were followed years later for monitoring. The kids, who did not eat the marshmallows versus those who ate them, had significant differences in their lives.

Those who had mastered their thoughts and replaced their thoughts with anything other than eating the marshmallows did better in school, got better jobs, and had better relationships. They learned the art of discipline and replacing.

Those who ate the marshmallows did not do as well; not only in test scores, but also in college and relationships. There is power is in the discipline of the mind… and the replacing.

There's definitely something to this.

RE-Member: "what you focus on you make room for."

Chapter 11

Kingdom, KingDOME and Frequency Hopping

Going back to the Bio-Field and our personal Bio-Field space: I am thinking about a famous actress name Hedy Lamarr. She was not only beautiFULL and talented as an actress, but she was an amazing inventor. A lot of people might not know about this; there are several documentaries on her and I have watched a few.

In a nutshell, during World War II, the Nazis were bombing our submarines and we were doing a careless job of bombing them back. We wasted a lot of ammo by missing a lot of shots. Hedy Lamarr came up with an invention where we could somehow lock our submarine on the frequency and/or code of "the enemy" submarine and sync our missiles to that energy field, lock into that code… and hit them without a miss.

Brilliant.

And it worked. With this technology, we finally started getting them every single time just by locking into their code within their frequency. The problem was, suddenly the same invention got into the hands of the 'enemy' and they started using it against us.

Uh-Oh.

So back to the drawing board: She went and came up with something called "frequency hopping" where basically we would scramble all of our code and frequency related to any instruments in our submarine so that "the enemy" couldn't lock onto us or our frequency.

The 'enemy' couldn't find us because of the scrambled field around our subs.

When I heard about this, all I could see in my mind's eye was a vision of our own Bio-Code field and how this works with the "KingDome". In my mind, I saw the Bio-Field as a "dome" around us, reflecting everything that we were thinking, feeling, or talking about. Get it? "King-dome/KingDome!?"

Immediately in my mind's eye I could see RE-Membering and RE-Minding union and all of the powerFULL I AM's that God is.

"I AM" John 8:58
"I AM who I AM" Exodus 3:14
"I am Alpha and Omega" (Jesus) Revelation 1:8
"I am from above" (Jesus) John 8:23
"I am God Almighty" Genesis 17:1
"I am He" John 18:5
"I am He who comforts you" Isaiah 51:12
"I am holy" 1Peter 1:16
"I am the door" (Jesus) John 10:9
"I am the door of the sheep" (Jesus) John 10:7
"I am the good shepherd" (Jesus) John 10:11
"I am the light of the world" (Jesus) John 9:5
"I am the bread of life" (Jesus) John 6:48
"I am the LORD, and there is no other" Isaiah 45:5
"I am the LORD who heals you" Exodus 15:26
"I am the LORD who makes all things" Isaiah 44:24
"I am the LORD, the God of all flesh" Jeremiah 32:27
"I am the LORD your God who divided the sea" Isaiah 51:15

"I am the LORD your God who teaches you to profit" Isaiah
48:17

"I am the LORD exercising loving-kindness, judgment, and
righteousness" Jeremiah 9:24

"I am the LORD, your Holy One" Isaiah 43:15

"I am the resurrection, and the life" (Jesus) John 11:25

"I am the root and offspring of David" (Jesus) Revelation
22:16

"I am the Son of God" (Jesus) John 10:36

"I am the vine" (Jesus) John 15:5

"I am the way, the truth, and the life" (Jesus) John 14:6

"I am their inheritance" Ezekiel 44:28

"I am their possession" Ezekiel 44:28

"I am your exceedingly great reward" Genesis 15:1

"I am your portion and your inheritance" Number 18:20

"I am your salvation" Psalm 35:3

"I am your shield" Genesis 15:1

"I am with you" Acts 18:10

"I am with you to deliver you" Jeremiah 1:8

"I am with you to save you" Jeremiah 30:11

"I am with you always" (Jesus) Matthew 28:20

I then saw an image of the Biblical names of God found in the Old and
New Testaments. The list also includes the names listed in the Hebrew
Scriptures and the New Testament Greek scriptures.

Advocate – 1 John 2:1

Adonai – Genesis 15:12

Almighty – Revelation 1:8

Alpha – Revelation 1:8

Amen – Revelation 3:14

Angel of the Lord – Genesis 16:7

Anointed One – Psalm 2:2

Apostle – Hebrews 3:1

Author and Perfecter of our Faith –
Hebrews 12:2

Beginning – Revelation 21:6

Bishop of Souls – 1 Peter 2:25

Branch – Zechariah 3:8

Bread of Life – John 6:35,48

Bridegroom – Matthew 9:15

Carpenter – Mark 6:3

Chief Shepherd – 1 Peter 5:4

The Christ – Matthew 1:16

Comforter – Jeremiah 8:18

Consolation of Israel – Luke 2:25

Cornerstone – Ephesians 2:20

Dayspring – Luke 1:78

Day Star – 2 Peter 1:19

Deliverer – Romans 11:26

Desire of Nations – Haggai 2:7
Emmanuel – Matthew 1:23
El Shaddaih (God is Mighty)
   – Genesis 49:24
End – Revelation 21:6
Everlasting Father – Isaiah 9:6
Faithful and True Witness
   – Revelation 3:14
First Fruits – 1 Corinthians 15:23
Foundation – Isaiah 28:16
Fountain – Zechariah 13:1
Friend of Sinners – Matthew 11:19
Gate for the Sheep – John 10:7
Gift of God – 2 Corinthians 9:15
God – John 1:1
Glory of God – Isaiah 60:1
Good Shepherd – John 10:11
Governor – Matthew 2:6
Great Shepherd – Hebrews 13:20
Guide – Psalm 48:14
Head of the Church – Colossians 1:18
Healer (Rapha) Exodus 15:26
High Priest – Hebrews 3:1
Holy One of Israel – Isaiah 41:14
Horn of Salvation – Luke 1:69
I Am – Exodus 3:14
Jehovah – Psalm 83:18
Jesus – Matthew 1:21
King of Israel – Matthew 27:42
King of Kings – 1 Timothy 6:15;
   Revelation 19:16
Lamb of God – John 1:29
Last Adam – 1 Corinthians 15:45
Life – John 11:25
Light of the World – John 8:12; John
   9:5
Lion of the Tribe of Judah
   – Revelation 5:5
Lord of Lords – 1 Timothy 6:15;

Revelation 19:16
Love – 1 John 4:7
Master – Matthew 23:8
Mediator – 1 Timothy 2:5
Messiah – John 1:41
Mighty God – Isaiah 9:6
Morning Star – Revelation 22:16
Nazarene – Matthew 2:23
Omega – Revelation 1:8
Passover Lamb – 1 Corinthians 5:7
Peace – (Yahweh-Shalom) Judges 6:24
Physician – Matthew 9:12
Potentate – 1 Timothy 6:15
Priest – Hebrews 4:15
Prince of Peace – Isaiah 9:6
Prophet – Acts 3:22
Propitiation – I John 2:2
Purifier – Malachi 3:3
Rabbi – John 1:49
Ransom – 1 Timothy 2:6
Redeemer – Isaiah 41:14
Refiner – Malachi 3:2
Refuge – Isaiah 25:4
Resurrection – John 11:25
Righteousness – Jeremiah 23:6
Rock – Deuteronomy 32:4
Root of David – Revelation 22:16
Rose of Sharon – Song of Solomon 2:1
Ruler of God's Creation
   – Revelation 3:14
Sacrifice – Ephesians 5:2
Savior – 2 Samuel 22:47; Luke 1:47
Second Adam – 1 Corinthians 15:47
Seed of Abraham – Galatians 3:16
Seed of David – 2 Timothy 2:8
Seed of the Woman – Genesis 3:15
Servant – Isaiah 42:1
Shepherd – 1 Peter 2:25
Shiloh – Genesis 49:10

Son of David – Matthew 15:22	Teacher – Matthew 26:18
Son of God – Luke 1:35	Truth – John 14:6
Son of Man – Matthew 18:11	Way – John 14:6
Son of Mary – Mark 6:3	Wonderful Counselor – Isaiah 9:6
Son of the Most High – Luke 1:32	Word – John 1:1
Stone – Isaiah 28:16	Vine – John 15:1
Sun of Righteousness – Malachi 4:2	Yahweh-Jireh (The Lord will Provide)
The God of SEEING – (El-Roi)	Genesis 22:14
Genesis 16:13	

Source is all of these things… and every one of these words and names carry a frequency wave.

And this is what's INSIDE US at any given, choice thought.

As we RE-Member and RE-Mind that we are in Union with each of these, the frequency goes out into the Bio-Field with the essence of each coded frequency scrambling the field.

The only thing that could lock in is a match… anything else could not penetrate.

This is truly Psalms 91.

> "He who dwells in the shelter of the Most High will remain secure and in rest in the shadow of the almighty whose power no enemy can with stand. I will say to the Lord, he is my refuge and my fortress. My God in him trust."

You could actually give the meanest "bad guy" your address and he wouldn't be able to find you… because you are invisible.

When we RE-Member and RE-Mind and STAY in UNION, we scramble the code, and frequency-hop our own DOME… and create a true KING-DOME around us in security.

And when it comes to Co-Creating Miracles on a moment to moment basis… you can guess that when we RE-Member and RE-Mind that all this is inside of us… and *we can only get a match*… we radiate out all the things of God and collect and/or magnetically suck in MORE of God things into our lives creating miracles.

We have the Choice to BE (in God and Source CODE) or not to be.

I hope this gives you a visual to your power. Let's move on to another in the next chapter as we continue to CREATE our Miracles now…

Chapter 12

Manifest Your Miracle Time!

So, how do we do it? You have waited this long! You have enough foundation. Now, this is where the rubber meets the road!

Now, I give credit in-part to Robert Tennyson Stevens for this diagram, whom I have already mentioned. However, because of my quantum and neuroscience background, I added some other pieces including some physics.

I gotta say, I woke up one morning and it was all *there.* Everything made sense. I was so excited I had to draw it out.

Dr. Sharnael Co-Creating

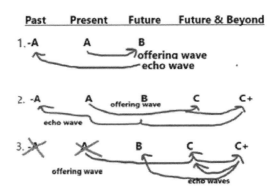

We have the past, the present, the future, the future and beyond.

-A is the past

A is the Present

B is the future

C is the Future and Beyond

C+ is even further.

To be Clear -A is any past negative belive or beliefs formed by scenarios or events from you and/or your generational DNA creating negative code.

Scenario 1

Let's say we're in the present—which is the "A." Since childhood, we have pretty much been under the programming of setting goals from A to B... In other words:

>We are in A; let's get to B.

>We are in A; let's get to B.

>We are in A; let's get to B.

That's the drill.

Whether it is becoming a cheerleader, getting good grades, or getting that job... we're told to sit in our current reality and write down our goals of getting to "B."

Therefore, the energy and the code of that is LITERALLY *getting to "B"*... which by definition, *isn't* B yet... *getting to "B" ISN'T BEING IN "B."*

We have been told to set goals to get to "B." Everything is about *reaching* the "B."

What this looks like energetically from a physics standpoint is if we are in "A," we put out the energy vibe or the "offering wave" out to "B." What happens next is "B" goes *back* in your *energetic timeline* with what is called an "echo wave" to not just the present "A" but the past "-A" to see where the energy belief systems really ARE.

Are there any snags energetically? Are there doubts within your MIND? WORDS? FEELINGS? ARE THERE SNAGS IN YOUR genetic programming from your ancestors subconsciously lowering your equations? Where are you *really*??

Where does your real belief lie?

If the offering wave goes back and there is a negative with a past issue whether it is genetic, a program or your doubts/fears of making cheerleader, getting a good grade or getting the job, this can cause a negative effect in the equation LITERALLY.

Scenario 2

You're still in "A" except this time you're offering wave goes all the way out to "C" or "C+" and beyond, the echo wave comes back to the "-A" which is your past to see if there's any snags there... even if there's a little drag you may land somewhere in the middle, maybe even at "B."

Scenario 3

You heal "-A." You do not associate with "-A." "-A" does not even exist in your world because you're in a new program of God in you and RE-Membering ALL the mighty things that Source is inside of you.

You're in the "A," you put out the offering to the future and beyond which is the "C" or "C+"... maybe all the way to "Z"?!? The echo wave comes back, checks for "-A"... nope... no "-A" to compromise the equation or to create any energetic snag.

It then checks into "A"... Wow. You ain't even there... because you are strong in "B," "C," or "C+" and beyond...

Then what happens? You land way out in the future... creating THAT code... and guess what... *you only get a match...*

Whatever you are... wherever you are... energetically... you only get a match.

What you focus on... you make room for.

In scripture this is where we, "Call those things that are not as though they are."

This is again where we get, "As a man/woman thinks in his/her HEART (energy magnet waves, beliefs waves, create photons to line up) so is he/she."

> Proverbs 29:18 KJV "Where *there is no vision*, the people perish." Get a God vision and HOLD IT!

> Colossians 3:2 "Fix your eyes, (the eyes of your heart) on things of Heaven (within)." That word "fix" means to "set" or to "observe and to direct the mind to..." in other words, STAY.

Again, To Be or not to Be... that is the Question...

THIS IS FREAKING AMAZING... Astonishing... This is Your Creative Power.

Chapter 13

Re-Coding Your Timeline

So, the next question you ask is "How do we get rid of the -A?" Great question. Let's chat about it. There are so many different ways to heal and/or transmute the "-A."

First of all, a biggie is RE-Membering and RE-Minding, of course, because nothing can separate you from the love of God but you. We'll go into that in another chapter.

And also REALizing the scripture Romans 12:2 that says

> "Do not be CON-Formed (con… deceit, trickery—formed… do not be formed or shaped by a con or trick…) by this world… but be trans-formed (meta-formed … meta meaning a change of position or condition. A metamorphosis) by the renewing of your mind.

When I looked up "world," I WAS SHOCKED. One of the meanings of that word "world" actually means *"timeline"* or **"age."**

Do not be CON-Formed to *the ages or timeline* of the culture or current reality… the "-A", "A" or even the stress of getting to "B" …But be Trans-Formed by the renewing of your mind. When I looked up "mind," it is the Greek 3563 in Strong's meaning: the perception or understanding of things.

Be transformed by the staying Power of God's timeline, and Creative forces at hand in Sources Creative abilities.

I hope you are getting this… because this is big y'all. *We make the Timeline…* we create the way.

Again, at one point I thought "things just happened to me" not realizing I was actually doing it myself…

Murphy's law states, *"Anything that can go wrong will go wrong."* Something terrible would happen, I would call three friends to all agree how terrible it was, and of course their response would be "Well… there's always something isn't there?" Meaning: a negative thing would *always* happen.

This is a program.

A sucky one.

And of course, getting folks to agree with me only proved I was right and just gave the program more energy to stay and grow and create more negative patterns.

I had another program I got from Doctor Phil that said, *"the best way to predict the future is to look at the past."* You know, look at the "-A"… and you'll know what to expect in the future…

Also, a sucky program.

Plus… *what you focus on you make room for.*

Then one day I saw a quote by Abraham Lincoln *"The best way to predict the future is to create it!"* ALAS! Honest Abe… THANK YOU! If anyone understood staying power, it was you!

Instead of the 'how bad things" always "happened to me" program,' how about, there's always something miraculous igniting in me. Everything good happens to me! I create miracles everywhere I go! As a matter of fact, I ignite miracles and everyone at contact!

These are some awesome programs and some great decrees. Decrees are one way to shift and heal the "-A" and "A" to "C+."

For time's sake, let me give you a list of other things that may help you to re-code. It may look very similar to what we talked about before in chapter 4:

> Grounding, Drinking water, Rest as required, Eat high vibe food, Essential Oils, Crystals, Sauna, Foot baths, Epsom salt baths, EMFs, Exercise, Fasting, Sunshine, Nature, Music, Art, Meditation/Prayer, Raindrop, Decrees, Outcome Mapping, treasure mapping, vison boards, Massage ... All of these contain high frequency vibes and code for recoding your shift in the energy and equation.

So, enjoy and start on this ASAP...

Side Note, Two things:

First—Essential Oils
With specifics to essential oils that actually contain frequency... I enjoy layering essential oils like frankincense, patchouli, wintergreen, cinnamon bark, peppermint, cistus, and of course rose (the highest frequency oils), and then layering it or anchoring it with more woodsy oils like cedarwood, balsam fir, Myrtle, spruce, white fir, etc. to ground it and anchor it in.

Second—Crystals
OK, don't get freaky on me. I promise you I am not weird. There's actually a science to this. If you would've told me this a few years ago, I would've laughed at you just like you're probably laughing now... but at this point maybe you're not laughing. Crystals work. God made them

for us. There is a science to it, and for those who believe in the bible they are actually biblical.

Crystals are structured from the stones themselves. They are not magic, but they do carry a vibration and a code specific to them in a structured form. It is transferable, and many feel it. Whether you feel it or not, the vibration still exists. Crystals form only in the right circumstances. It has everything to do with high temperatures, gasses, and the earth's crust. As they cool themselves, they randomly arrange the constituent atoms to a more stable relationship. This effect has a three-dimensional repeating pattern known as 'crystal lattices' in which every atom has found the most stable balance arrangement possible; crystals then continue to grow in whatever conditions.

Even if crystals are exposed to chaos, they have the ability and stability to keep their structure. So, think about it: we may be in an environment of chaos or we may be ourselves in a chaotic state, but when we add something stable to our Bio-Field and/or our body, specifically on our skin, it creates a calming effect as well as a reprogramming effect. Each individual crystal has its own unique vibration and support to us. There is a huge range of different crystals and minerals and gemstones that are all God-given to us for our best, higher self. Using crystals and/ or introducing crystals to our body in whatever state we're in brings a sense of order and balance, not only physically, and emotionally, but also mentally.

They are very effective and very healing. I have been studying this subject, and I have interviewed several people. There are specific crystals to even help transmute addictions, shift negative programs to positive ones, and eliminate stress. I have compiled a personal list of specific crystals and stones that have helped me and many others I know. This will help you if you are interested. To give you more understanding of this topic, I have a *Crystals, Oils and Energy* group. It is a yearly membership[g] that is available to you. This group has hundreds of posts, videos, and several classes all based on the subject of crystals, oils, and energy support. I also have a flash card set for educational purposes that is available on my website at *www.swiftfire.org*. I know you will enjoy both. The cards are called, *"Crystals, Oils and Decrees.*[h]" There are 80 cards of inspiration to raise your vibration and manifest your miracles now!

All these things serve a greater, higher, function and purpose, and all of them can help press the "reset button" not only to our energetic Bio-Fields but also to our mental and Spiritual programming.

Top Crystals for Addictions and or Changing Programs

Hematite
Amethyst
Carnelian
Clear Quartz
Tiger eye
Rose Quartz
Citrine
Black Obsidian
Howlite
Amber

---

g   Class information can be found at www.swiftfire.org/onlineclasses
h   Available for purchase at www.swiftfire.org/store

Chapter 14

The Royal Law

See, we are not "punished" *for* our sins we are merely receivers of the consequences of our own choices! "Karma" is an electric transaction made by our own choices. Our own creations.

The wages (cost) of sin is death... death isn't only death like dying... this death is death of consciousness... it's "Thanatos," separation of Life and Salvation in God."

The word "salvation" in Hebrew 3444 is: deliverance, help, prosperity, salvation, SECURITY and VICTORY!

Sin is just falling short of the highest PERSONAL target. The code of "missing the target" sends an electronic signal out in radiation, and then magnetizes a match back.

That match is our own "wage," or cost. "HE" doesn't assign the punishment. It's the law. It's the way energy works in the earth field.

God knows the law! This is why God gently reminds us to MAKE OUR HIGHEST CHOICES moment-to-moment.

There are basic "sins" but everyone has a unique personal path custom-designed for them, and being True to that path keeps us 'clear' of any "bad" transactions. We have basic 10 commandments set in the Old Testament.

The second commandment says "Love your neighbor as yourself."

Then the New Testament introduces something even higher... The Royal Law.

The Royal Law is John 13:34, "A new command I give to you, Love One another. As I have loved you, so must you love one another.

Meaning:

A. We must Love ourselves. Period. God is Love. (This may seem opposite in ministry or service type professions. It may even seem opposite as parents or in marriage)... but secure your "oxygen mask" first. Thrive in your life FIRST.)

    Why? SELF. It says in both commandments to love YOURSELF and Love one another... including self. Love is critical. When we follow the Royal Law, loving ourselves and others AS GOD LOVES US we get a match transaction!

    People who are 'asleep' only submit to our lowest frequency. If we are less than love, guess what? You get a match! The law doesn't take a day off.

    1 John 1:4 "Beloved, let us love one another for God is love."

    God is Love. God is IN us. When we step outside Union we fall short of the target, or "sin."

B. When we Truly love ourselves, we easily love others because they ARE us. They are just a mirror. We share the image of our God and we share a unified field... making these transactions automatic.

    We are not "punished" for our sins. We are receivers of our own transactions or our creations.

    Every morning, I take the kids to the bus for school. I used to say, "Have a great day!" The last few weeks I felt almost like it was wrong to say it that way and then I would quickly change it to "MAKE it a great day!"

I woke up hearing this scripture: "This is the day that the Lord has made... I will rejoice and be glad in it." Psalms 118:24

"Has made" is, "ASHA" to fashion, to do, to accomplish, to be produced... to make offering, to put in order... to bring about... to make/create. It does not mean *has made*... as in, already done... but *in progress*.

Every day God in Us fashions, produces, and brings about our day... (The Kingdom of God is within. Then we radiate the KINGDOME of God as our realm Bio-Field...Christ in me Hope of Glory!)

Our day is not preset, it's IN production and no one "outside" creates our day. WE do. We, God IN ME, God in YOU... do this—our choice, our creation... moment-to-moment. Make today Great!

Let's look at this one in Revelations 21:5:

"The One seated on the throne said, 'Behold, I make all things new.' Then he said, 'write this down for these words are FaithFULL and TRUE."

The beginning part of this scripture says, "The One (3588 including the feminine One... look it up).

"The One Seated on the Throne..."

What is throne? Where is the Throne? The Heart. The I AM coming from the heart. A place of power... dominion (Kingdom/KingDome).

Throne G2362 "Meton," power or DOMinion! (Dome)

And We, (in Union) are seated in "heavenly places" within. A higher realm, a higher dimension (or octave), a higher sound, a place of higher

God perspective, a place of AUTHORITY. Look at the word "authority." It has the word "author" in it...we authors create!

Behold, (BE FIRM... HOLD this) I (me and God) make ALL things *new*!!!

The word "new" means "kainos" G2537, new in quality, innovation, FRESH in development, of opportunity; new because it is NOT found exactly like this before!" PowerFULL!

Behold! again, "I make all things NEW! Not I WILL make all things new... but I MAKE all things new..."

Then he said, "WRITE these things down for these are faithful and TRUE!" God thought it was so important or he wouldn't have said this.

When we RE-Member to STAY on our throne, in heavenly places IN GOD in our heart, we are The Kingdom and we create the KINGDOME making all things new... creating, fashioning our day moment to moment...

When we RE-Member and RE-Mind and STAY in UNION, we scramble the code, and frequency-hop our own DOME... and create a true KING-DOME around us in security AND only get a MATCH TO KINGDOM THINGS... **LOVE**.

When it comes to Co-Creating Miracles on a moment-to-moment basis... when we RE-Member and RE-Mind that all this is inside of us and all *WHO* is inside of US... and *we can only get a match*... we radiate out all the things of God and collect and/or magnetically suck in MORE of God things into our lives creating miracles.

We have the Choice to BE (in God and Source CODE) or not to be...

I hope this gives you a new perspective to your power. Let's move on to another in the next chapter as we continue to CREATE our Miracles now...

Chapter 15

Probabilities versus Standing Waves

There are multiple timelines of probabilities for you. With each of your choices, the entire timeline shifts to something new. This is why staying in UNION with RE-Membering and RE-Minding is so important. We're sending out the code of God to get our highest choice magnetized back to us at all times.

> Seek first the *Kingdom (Kingdome)* of God, and *then* all these things will be added unto you. (Matthew 6:33)

Have you ever heard of probability waves? These waves look like spirals twirling and pulsating, coming out of your body into your Bio-Field. They expand and contract, expand and contract, expand and contract, kind of like birth. With each choice, you are birthing something new. With each choice you're not only shifting your timeline but you're shifting everyone around you because of the well-known butterfly effect.

The butterfly effect, with reference to the chaos theory, is the phenomenon where a minute, localized change in a complex system can have large effects elsewhere.

This means every single thing that we do affects everybody. A single small change in one state can result in a large difference in a later state. A very small change in an initial condition has significantly different outcomes in not only you but also everyone.

We may not realize we're shifting the world... but with every thought, every feeling, every word and every choice, we are truly doing *just that*. As you shift your Bio-Field from the inside out, your electric belt shifts, which affects the entire world. EVERYTHING is an INSIDE JOB... and as we shift, everyone that touches the hem of your electric "garment" shifts with us.

Because of this, STAYING power is vastly IMPORTANT.

What is Staying Power?

Think about Peter in the scriptures. Jesus said to the disciples, "Who do they say I am?" Peter replied, "You're the Messiah!"

Jesus was excited and said, "You could have only got that info from the INNER!"... and yet two sentences later, Jesus had to say to the same guy, "Stop thinking that thought form."

Yikes.

Just like Peter... we can "Peter out" of staying power in the RE-Member and RE-Mind aspect. Or we can RE-Member, RE-Mind and STAY.

I AM already Loved... and Stay. I am Secure, and I STAY. I am Miraculous, and I Stay.

This brings me to what's called "the standing wave." By definition, a standing wave is: a vibration of a system in which some particular point remains *fixed* while others between them vibrate with the maximum amplitude.

Here we go again...

> Philippians 4:8 says, '*Fix* your mind or set your mind on *these* things... thing that are pure, lovely, good news, etc.' as discussed previously.

A standing wave looks like one long, steady, constant wave going out...

When I think of the standing wave I think of the scripture in Ephesians 6:13, "Therefore take up the full armor of God (The KINGDOME Bio-Field), so that when the day of evil comes you will be able to stand your ground and having done everything to STAND."

That word "stand" is the G2476 which is a prolonged form of standing still, standing firm, and standing ready to be established; to set in balance.

I. Love. This. Don't You?

Are you getting all this? As we stand in LOVE who is God… we radiate out God's love, and we start a ripple effect shifting our world from the inside out.

The Kingdom of God is within… Yes, Christ IN me, Hope of Glory AND Source, is *in* EVERYTHING…

> Colossians 1:17, "He is before all things, and in Source, all things hold together."

> Romans 11:36, "For from Source all things originate, and through Source all things living exist and to Source are all things directed."

As long as WE RE-Member and RE-Mind and STAY… our staying power creates miracles, not just for us, but THROUGH US.

Let's Stay in Love with everything we create!

Chapter 16

Trauma Loops and Signature Codes

In this season of your new awakening and shifting the codes and equations for your perfect miracles, I invite you to be aware of a process that sometimes can occur. I call it "Trauma Loops," specially having to do with your signature codes and cyclical times.

I'll just give you a real world example, so you can have an anchor to hold onto. Last September during 9/11, we were in meetings to recode the times.

Specifically, because it was 9/11, I made a point not to watch anything on television, see anything on social media or anything to do with the whole 9/11 event. By that time, 9/11 had happened 17 years prior, but the media still loved igniting a reboot in us, usually with continuous scenes from that day played over and over and over.

Please understand there is code to this. There are programs of fear and trauma looking to loop in your signature code and entice you to its sound.

There are even codes to different things like memorials, places that carry resonance of the fear and pain. These codes and images keep the trauma going.

I invite you to stay out of these trauma loops trying to loop you back into the programs.

Obviously, the only trauma loop in the world isn't just 9/11, that's a big one of course, but you may have your versions of several smaller ones that are more personal and unique to you. The "news" in general isnt the best source of good vibes.

There is a code to it; frequency and sound are looking for entrance. If there is any residue in the signature code, it can hook in, creating old patterns to emerge and reboot.

You will use anyone and anything to "test" yourself... meaning you create it to come to you, to test you. Anything that shows up in your world less than God, is really you pushed out... you're showing up in others to show you what's still there.

Anyone and anything "sleepy" will submit to your lowest frequency and illusion about yourself and look for ways to reboot you back to the negative.

Any awake person will see you as God sees you. A sleepy person or situation will ONLY submit to your "lowest" illusion.

Bob Jones, a spiritual father to me, once came to me in a dream and said, "Don't drink the wine."

I responded, "Don't drink the wine? Like real wine? Alcohol?" and he said, "No. Do not submit to lower frequencies."

That being said, back to the 9/11 example: I made a point like, 'hey I am not really going to connect with that, I am not getting entangled with that, I am going to take a moment to be off of social media and the news because I knew there would be such an attempt to reboot into that system and to bring me back into it.'

Your consciousness and your imagination are really, really powerFULL, and the media wants to use your creative power to co-create, because if your focus is on those kinds of things in those kinds of events, then you will "image" that and you will project that.

On a conscious, collective level if we're all imaging and projecting that, we not only feel all those things in our bodies as if it is happening "now" (because our limbic system cannot tell the difference between what goes on in reality versus what's on a screen) AND because those things are "happening" now we're "imaging-a-nation" in fear because we're connecting with the fear, the sorrow, and the pain of those things that happen.

That "imaging" creates an open doorway for us to get a match and to create more trauma and more things to occur.

Oh no...

This is why in scripture it says to "sweep the house clean and keep it clean" (Luke 11:25).

I hope that makes sense.

So back to the 9/11 situation: in the process, I had made a point that I wasn't going to entertain that, I chose not to engage in that. For you do whatever you choose, but for me this was going to be a time for me to *re-code* the day. I was going to re-code 9/11 into a new code of something that was positive, pivotal, brand-new, awesome, and beautiFULL; a rebirthing.

That's the kind of code that I was going for. As a group, we had people from several different states and cities meeting up to do just that. Together prophetically and electrically, this was our mission for the day.

As we were recoding, we were focusing on gratitude, love, and peace. While this was going on, it was interesting because this girl in our group got an opportunity to go meet with someone from her past who lived in this particular city. Apparently, at one time, she lived there but had moved away because of some trauma related things. This person who wanted to meet with her was not necessarily a bad or a good person, but she apparently had connected that trauma and time period to this city; even that timeline of trauma related things.

They were going to go grab lunch the next day, but we were awake, RECODING until 3:00 in the morning. She ended up sleeping through her alarm clock and was not able to meet up with this person. She was very, very upset that she missed out. Upset, she contacted me asking for prayer and for victory in her emotions due to missing out on the opportunity.

Now, you know me. I am a person of my word and I like to follow through with what I say, and she definitely has integrity. It's a big deal to be integrated and to do what you say you're going to do. It's important to integrity and keeping commitments.

And she felt really, really bad about it. She couldn't go back and fix it. She was having a hard time forgiving herself and moving on for some reason.

Suddenly, I knew what happened. My response to her was this, "Hey, you know, first off, I guess your body needed the sleep—and secondly, you were *not supposed* to meet with this person." She knew I was right.

Again, the signature code of this girl had unhealed residue. She used this person to show up, looking to hook her in, and back to the old patterns and trauma loops.

Her body knew not to go in yet until the loop was completely healed.

Once healed? No problem.

Just something to be awakened to and aware of. Keep the house clean and take all the time required to heal in this process for everyone's sake. This avoids rebooting the trauma loops.

Chapter 17

It's Time to Meet Will

Back in 2009, I was dealing with some pretty crazy health issues. At the time I had these recurring dreams where I heard: it is time to meet Will, it is time to meet Will, it is time to meet Will.

Each and every time, I would come out of my dream wondering who in the heck Will was. I contacted the people in my office and inquired if there's anything on the schedule of a specific church or group or person I had an appointment with named Will.

There was not anyone.

I thought, well maybe there's a William or Bill or Billy. Nothing came up.

Weeks later I was doing some ministry meetings and met a woman who had found out about my health issues. She encouraged me to go see a man named 'Doctor Lucky.' I was not entirely thrilled about it to be honest, because I had been to doctors for over six years and never really felt that it had proved to be beneficial. I had been given over thirty different prescriptions and all of them seemed to just give me more side effects, which in turn, just gave me more problems, so on and so on.

I had a small suitcase of different meds that I was taking as I would travel.

There was a mental gymnastics aspect to the whole thing because there were different instructions and rules for all of them such as: one pill could only be taken with water, another should be taken with milk. Another I had to take with a full meal, a different one in the morning, another two at night. I had charts and maps and all kinds of things to figure it out. It was awful. Worse than that, I wasn't even feeling better. And not one of them could tell me what was wrong.

This woman finally talked me into going to see this medical doctor, this… 'Dr. Lucky.[i]'

That alone was pretty interesting.

He had many different types of machines from various countries: Russia, China, and Germany. He is all about frequency, all of it was helpful, and he did cutting-edge things I had never even heard of or been exposed to before.

At one point during my appointment with him, which by the way was about six hours long, he had me hooked up to a machine. He used a process called muscle testing. Muscle testing is absolutely incredible. It is something I really encourage you to dig into deeper if you don't know anything about it. I have a membership class[j] that teaches everything on the Biblical and scientific aspects of muscle testing[k].

While we were sitting there in his office, he handed me a piece of paper. As soon as I laid hands on the piece of paper, I heard a sound similar to when PAC-MAN dies in the video game. It was not a good sound.

---

i   Dr. Lucky is founder and CEO of The Flowood Lifestyle and Wellness Clinic. He is a pastoral health coach, minister, teacher, author and speaker. He has been a champion of wholistic healthcare for twenty years.

j   Class information can be found at www.swiftfire.org/onlineclasses

k   Class information can be found at www.swiftfire.org/onlineclasses

I could tell by Dr. Lucky's face that he was pretty concerned about the sound as well. It is not the face you want to see whenever you're looking at your doctor.

I had not even looked at what was written on the paper. I merely touched it, and it made that sound.

He scratched his head and looked really freaked out.

He even made the kind of face you don't want to see your doctor make. He even made the comment, "Well, that never happens!!!!"

That did not worry me at all. Not!

When I finally looked at the paper, I saw that it was filled with all kinds of beautiFULL decrees such as: you are loved, you're beautiFULL, you have an awesome purpose, everybody loves you, you have a destiny.

I couldn't understand what was going on.

I asked him, "What is this about? I don't understand?

He said, "Your body did not come into agreement with anything that was on the paper. Not a single thing."

My mind went in circles because I couldn't figure out what this meant. I mean, I did not want to tell him that I was in full time ministry and that I literally I taught this all over the world. What kind of representation could I possibly be for Christ if I did not believe any of this myself?

I was mortified. And I was absolutely scared that the next question he would ask me was: "What do you do for a living anyway?"

I was absolutely prepared to respond with: *I am a pro-bowler.*

With the intent not to embarrass God.

I said: "What do we do now?"

He scratched his head like he was trying to figure it out himself. He said he had never seen anything like this before.

Super comforting, I thought.

He took the piece of paper from my hand, and he walked out of the room for a minute. When he came back with a pencil, I saw him writing something on the top of the paper before he handed it back to me. As soon as he did, thank God the machine did not make the noises again. It did not make any noise at all actually.

I looked at the top of the paper to see what in the world he had written. I did not see anything really different except in pencil at the very top it said: **I will**.

I looked up, a bit confused. I asked: "Can you explain what's going on please?"

He said, "I want you to take that piece of paper and in front of every one of those statements I want you to insert: *'I will.'*"

For example:

> *I will* that I am loved.
> *I will* that I am beautiful.
> *I will* that I have a destiny
> *I will* that everyone loves me… And so on…

He continued, "Every day for the next thirty days, I want you to get in front of the mirror. Then repeat these things to yourself with eye contact over and over until you completely believe it. Until everything is in alignment."

He said, "Your will is 400,000 times stronger than your spirit."

As soon as he said that, all I could hear going on inside me was: *"It is time to meet Will. It is time to meet Will."*

See, we have the power to make choices. You, personally, can do all the things that you do either way. But we have a God Positioning System (GPS) that's internally guiding us towards our HIGHEST CHOICE. We can override anything the GPS says with our will and our choices. But if it isn't God's highest choice, then that's not the best synergy out there. Anything less than what's really "True" records as a "lie" and we get a "match" to that. (More on this in the next chapter.)

Or we can pay attention to that GPS and follow our hearts to do what is our highest at every given moment. Let's invest in the time that we have here and be the shiniest version of ourselves. The reason why we're here, by the way, is to be Light and Love to make a difference and create cool stuff.

We all have the choice to make.

I invite you to look over all things that you're doing and ask yourself: "Why? What's the motivation? What's the agenda?"

It is time for you to really take some internal, deep thoughts and evaluate where you are and where you're going. Are you on *your* timeline, or are you on God's timeline?

Are you just coasting through life, or is every day a miracle? Are you just going through the daily motions to get done and to get through it? Barely surviving? Or are you living your miraculous, amazing, *credible* Light-Life, moment-to-moment for you, for God, for yourself, and for everybody?

This next chapter is a biggie.

Chapter 18

True

This next part of my testimony was and still IS pivotal for me. Some of you may have never had any kind of experience like this, I may have been skeptical, "What? OK, whatever."

And for some of you this is just pretty normal.

Either way, you can tell me that you believe it happened or don't believe it. It will not make it go away, and it will not take away from the fact that it really *happened,* and it is *true.*

To this day I get emotional every single time I talk about it.

A little bit after the appointment with Dr. Lucky, I went home and continued living my life, starting with the things he said to do physically to support my body.

A few days after, when I woke up, I walked into my living room. It did not look much like my living room used to, and there were two very, very tall beings of light in the living room standing there like they had been waiting for me.

These beings were absolutely beautiFULL! Their skin that was not really skin, it was more like iridescent light.

They stood very tall, their stature itself seemed to demand respect, yet they were not demanding respect outwardly. They were not trying to be intimidating but, wow, the feelings within were intense. My heart was racing. Their vibration coming from them was beyond anything I had felt up to then.

The feeling coming from them was absolute love, and yet it literally scared the poo outta me.

There was also a very ancient-looking desk, and there were stacks and stacks of books everywhere I looked. I knew intuitively that they were records of a lot of different things.

There were hundreds, if not thousands, of books all over the living room. One of the big beings walked over and sat behind the desk, opened a book started going through the pages.

I had absolutely no understanding, but something inside me said to go look and see what this 'being' was looking at. I walked around behind the desk and looked around his (or its) very enormous shoulder. I could see what was written in the books. Written within were records, tons and tons of records that I cannot go into publicly, but it was like an accounting system of different dates, different times, and different ways that people were healed of many things.

The more that I read those records as I scanned through the pages, the more something was shifting inside of me. I could feel myself e-x-p-a-n-d, specifically from my heart region. I felt this pulsation/sound/vibration or frequency. I choose words to explain this to you, but I could feel this enlargement, this... radiation coming out and going through my entire body. I felt lighter. I felt different. It felt... bigger. I felt like Love was touching every bit of who I was inside and out. Every single cell in my body felt it. All of my organs, all of my blood, even my hair; it was an upgrade. It was a tune up. It was... I don't have words to express what was happening.

In my thoughts, I became aware that they already knew what I was thinking just by the way they were responding to what I didn't say, but was merely thinking. I knew what they were thinking too, but they never spoke out loud to me.

One looked more masculine. The other looked iridescent and was an incredibly beautiFULL, ancient, (yet not ancient?) Scandinavian-type woman.

I knew her as 'True.' I am crying now even writing this. Every time I talk about this I get that same feeling that I was there. That moment changed everything.

For some reason, it felt as though I had a memory of her or maybe that I had known her all along.

One of them looked at me and said in their mind: "What do you want?"

Before I could form the words... I heard my insides say "I wanna be a part of that." (Regarding the book.)

The book was shut, and they looked at each other like: "Well, okay then."

One even kinda shrugged his shoulders like "uhhh... okay."

I felt something even bigger inside of me at that moment, and I still don't have the words to explain it fully. I felt like light went through my entire body and was radiating out. Could I ever look as shiny and radiant as they did? Could it be that I could be a part of something so big for all these people in the books? All these people who were healed? Could I be a part of that?

For some reason, I knew they were about to leave and that my time with them was very short.

I wanted it to last forever, and I never wanted them to leave. True looked at me like she knew she had to go. She came closer to me and looked at my face and she said something I'll never forget for the rest of my life.

She said, "Make sure to tell them *'You're not truly living unless you're living true.'*"

Everything inside of me shook and echoed.

The emotion that I had in that moment was overpowering. Even now as I write this, with tears streaming down my face I can feel that same feeling. It makes me emotional every time.

"You're not *truly* living unless you're *living true*."

I knew that meant so many things. Such a simple statement meant everything to me.

I mean everything.

They were gone.

The books were gone.

The desk was gone.

Everything disappeared except for my normal living room.

My science brain couldn't even contain what had just happened.

My body was vibrating.

I could barely speak or even put together the experience I just had.

All I could think and hear inside of me was:

You're not truly living unless you're living true.

You're not truly living unless you're living true.

You're not truly living unless you're living true.

So true.

Living *True* is doing everything you're supposed to do while you're here in the time that you have been given.

Living True is living well, loving well.

Living True is being in the right job, working with the right people, being with the right partner, going to all the right places, moment to moment and every given day in any given year.

> John 8:32 says, "You shall **know** the Truth, and the Truth shall set you free."

> The word 'know' is the G1097 to perceive, to understand, to be very intimate.

Living True is living in integrity. That word "integrity" is interesting. It means to be INTEGRATED, mind - body - spirit, in harmony. Integration is key in living. Not just for your own life and health and patterns but for all in the unified field... which is EVERYONE.

Think of Job in the Bible. Scriptures say it was "his *integrity* that was his protection." RE-Member the 1500 positive chemicals you create when *Living True*? This affects both your body and the Bio-Field and the unified field of people on the earth.

Living true is listening to that GPS inside: that God Positioning System that's internal, that's real, that's custom to you in your life.

It has absolutely nothing to do with what anyone *expects* you to do.

As a matter fact, you may be asked or called to do things no other person on this earth is called to do.

It may look crazy to everybody.

You may look crazy to everybody.

Doesn't matter though, does it?

It only matters that you're true to *you* and to *God inside of you.*

Everything you do, everything you say, everywhere you go, everyone you talk to, everyone you don't talk to, everything matters...

We all have choices, and we all have free will. God did not make us robots to do everything perfectly the way he wanted us to. He gave us the choice and the will to do exactly what we are called to in the time we have here.

We get to listen to the internal energy center within... and no matter the "reality," create the way there. Hack the miracle place. Look in the future, be that energy and bring it to us.

Create our way.

Be the True Miracle we are.

All of the dreams inside of you are NOT made up.

They are real. They are important to the world.

They are unique and specific to you.

No one on the planet can be you.

No one knows what you know.

No one has the skill set you do or the make up or experience that you do.

Not a single person could express or communicate the way you do, in the way you do, with the sound and frequency you carry.

You are you. And you're pretty freaking good at it when you choose to be.

You're making stuff anyway. You might as well make cool stuff, right?

And get this…

All the knowledge in the world is already *here*.

All the dreams, inventions, songs, poems, books, science, love, money everything is here… we just have to RE-Member that we already have access to it because it is inside of us. Source who knows it all, is inside of is inside of *US*.

In Purity.

How do we access this, you ask? How do we tune-in?

He who has ears to hear and eyes to see… the answers are already here.

Before you have asked, I have answered. (Isaiah 65:24)

As we awaken and come to RE-Membering God WHO IS ALL KNOWING and ALL UNDERSTANDING AND ALL CREATION, we have everything that is already required. It is just doing it. In action.

I AM God in action now.

It only takes us getting quiet, really listening, not just speaking or wait- ing to speak… listening… feeling and then receiving the plan. And honestly, you already know. It is usually "hidden" in plain sight.

Receive with your receiver.

This is how we RE-Member.

Every "thing" currently created actually came from the "place." Source then created twice through "us". We conceive in our heart and mind first, then manifest in the physical.

What we receive, we can conceive and what we can imagine or conceive in our heart and mind we can conceive and give birth to.

No matter WHAT it is.

We are always creating, one way or another.

What are you receiving, conceiving, and creating today?

Everything already exists on the inside. Go find it... and then CREATE IT.

The whole universe is waiting.

(Make cool stuff please.)

Chapter 19

To Be or Not to Be

RE-Member: You are a Created, Loving, Light-Being, Spirit-guided by the power INSIDE of you and this GPS.

External forces are nothing. Internal ETERNAL forces are EVERYTHING.

There are consequences of believing the power is outside of you. If you believe this "power" is on the outside or belongs to someone else, then that thing will hold dominion over you (dome-minion… which are you moving into and from? KingDome or…?)

No one has control over you and your thoughts or behaviors. No one can "make you" feel sad, bad, fear, anger, whatever… do not give away your power so easily.

The discipline is in the MIND and Heart of RE-Membering and RE-Minding (perception of heart and mind). You are God's Highest Form of Creation! Your mind is a Divine Center of Operation! I AM the Mind of Christ, and I Stay.

If we will not fast from the world (Perception… external culture and timeline), we will not find God's Kingdom or KingDome. Psalms 91… the God Bio-Field.

We will not find God's Domain or Dome-Main. *Main* in Latin is to "Stay" as in re-main, to main again.

In other words, "THE KINGDOM DOMAIN" is the 'KING DOME.' SO STAY.'

It is a choice. To be, or not to BE.

We can BE and RE-Member our power and God's KingDome, or let (the perception of the eternal culture and timeline... dominion, dome-minion) happen to us. A "minion" is one that is less than... who follows.

Who are you "following?" God's GPS (God Positioning System within), or external chatter/world programming? I prefer Sovereign KingDome authority over perception of "world" external powers and timelines.

I AM the Mind of Christ. I AM God PowerFULL.

Everything else? YOU MOVE!

Chapter 20

Miracles Happen

John 10:9 (NASB) says, "I am the door; if anyone enters through Me, he will be saved, and will go in and out and find pasture."

That word "door" means, "portal, gate or opportunity."

The word "pasture" means, "met with growth, increase, feeding."

God is LOVE. And Love is the Door. As we enter Love and Truth (who is God) and as we walk in love and continue to perceive love in everything, we have increase. We have miracles.

Jesus walked in many miracles. Many were recorded, and volumes of miracles were not even recorded in the Bible (John 20:30). And, get this! He left us the promise that we can do greater things than these (John 14:12-14).

Greater things than Jesus? Geez. For real? That's BIG!

I'll give you three examples of the kind of miracles we are capable of when we walk in Love... or God.

Miracle Example #1

One day I was sitting at my desk in my office with my daughter, and I was making an acronym with the word "Love" and "I AMs." So far, I had:

I Am:

    L- Light
    O- (blank)
    V-Vibration
    E- Energy

I was trying to think of a word to fit my "O." I texted a group of my friends and asked, "Hey! What's a God word for O?" Someone replied, "Oils." Hmmmm… that was not it.

While working on this, the phone rang. I noticed the number was familiar. This same number had called 4-5 times previously leaving messages on my voicemail.

The messages were from a lady claiming she had met me at a conference. She described how the two of us had been talking at this conference, but then someone "whisked me away, and we did not get to finish our conversation." (She wanted to finish our conversation on the phone.)

The "problem" was, I was not at that conference. I was actually at home in Montana at the time. I never called her back because I thought it was the wrong number and that she meant to call someone else.

The calls became more persistent and the details were getting more specific. I did not call back because I did not choose to embarrass her. And honestly, I thought she would maybe realize the mistake and quit calling.

But… she did not quit calling.

Here I was, making this acronym and this new call comes through. "Dr. Sharnael, please call me, I'd love to finish our conversation, I really need your help."

My daughter says to me, "Mom she's not gonna quit calling, you're gonna have to tell her."

So, I picked up the phone. She went into the same thing she had said previously on voicemail… and then I stopped her and said kindly, "Hey, thank you so much for calling but I think you have me confused with someone else."

She said, "What do you mean?"

I said, "I was not *at* that conference. I was in Montana that weekend."

She said, "Well, I don't know what to say, you must be mistaken, you talked to me!"

I said, "I apologize. I am sure there is some explanation to this."

She said, "This *is* Dr. Sharnael with me on the phone right now, correct?"

I said, "Yes."

She said, "Are you a naturopathic doctor?"

I said, "Yes."

She said, "You specialize in aromatherapy, right?"

I said, "Yes."

She asks, "And your ministry name is Swiftfire International, right?"

I said, "Yes."

She said, "And you know Ian Clayton[1], right?" (a guy I have done ministry with many times.)

I said, "Yes, ma'am."

---

1   Ian Clayton, founder of Sons of Thunder, teaches that intimacy is about the 'passionate pursuit of the person of God' and doing things with him because you want to not because you have to.

She said, "It was **you**... *you* talked to me. Then, someone came over in the middle of us talking and started to whisk you away to the green room. You took out a piece of paper and wrote down your number and gave it to me. You asked me to call you at your office because we did not get to finish our conversation!"

I said, "I am sure there is a reasonable resolve to this... maybe someone there looked like me?? Maybe? What did she look like?"

Her reply was in FULL frustration now, "SHE LOOKED LIKE *YOU* BECAUSE IT WAS *YOU!*"

WOW... I took a breath and started to explain how wrong she was... then I looked down at my paper and heard the word that made me literally tremble inside.

"Omnipresent."

OMG.

Omnipresent.

I AM Omnipresent.

I was motionless. I hadn't been able to think of a word before.

OMNIPRESENT! ME?!

Instantly, I was in disbelief and then heard the phrase, "You can do GREATER THINGS THAN THESE!" "You can do all things through Jesus." (The door, gate, opportunity.)

GEEZ.

ME!

Yes me, and yes You!

I said to her, "Yes, ma'am, forgive me, that definitely was me. Let's finish our conversation... how can I help?"

She explained what she needed. I actually had the answers to help. And she was helped.

See, God will use you in ALL KIND OF WAYS when you are open to TRUTH, LOVE, INCREASE and MIRACLES. Yes, even in transportation or bi-locating. This is my inheritance. This takes multitasking to a new level!

You have the same capability in SOURCE. Everything is frequency, and the highest frequency is God or love. This is the door to OPPORTUNITY and MIRACLES.

Acts 8:26-40 speaks of Philip leading an Ethiopian to Christ. After the eunuch was baptized, "the Spirit of the Lord took him away, and the eunuch did not see him again, but went away rejoicing. Philip, however, appeared at Azotus."

This is more of a definition of teleporting not bi-locating. But this is our inheritance, too. We get to do GREATER things than these... God defied the laws. And, so can we when we enter that "door" of opportunity through LOVE.

Miracle Example #2

I had a set of wrist weights I'd wear through the day as I worked... and especially when I worked out. I was on my way to go out of town to speak at a conference, so I was packing. When I looked for my wrist weights for some reason I couldn't find them. I backtracked in my mind to see if I could remember where I had them last. I asked my family to help me look for them. We looked for over an hour... all around the house... the car... everywhere.

I knew I had to sit still and get quiet.

I RE-Member sitting and saying out loud, "I AM God's Mind RE-Membering where my wrist weights are." I have done this many times and have usually found whatever it is, instantaneously when I actually RE-Membered to do it.

Suddenly, I had a mental picture "seeing them."

I had them at the gym! Mentally I could see myself taking off the wrist weights as I was getting on a scale because I did not want my scale to measure the extra weight. When I took them off, I put them on this ledge that was next to the scale. Then I saw them in my mind's eye *still* sitting on that ledge.

I called the gym and asked the front desk if they could please go over to that ledge in the other room and get my arm weights and put them behind the desk so I could come by and pick them up.

She told me that another person who was working there had actually found them exactly where I "saw" them already, and that she had them in her possession, but the girl had gone home from work. She assured me that she would call her and tell her to make sure to bring them back tomorrow for me to pick them up. Later, she called me back and explained that the lady would bring them back in the morning.

Well, at least they were "found."

But my flight was at six in the morning, so there was no way I was going to be able to get them before I left on my trip.

Bummer.

I RE-Member going to sleep that night imagining that I already had my wrist weights NOW.

I asked myself "Now that you *already have* your wrist weights with you **right now,** what's new and different for you?" I imagined me already having my wrist weights in my possession currently. I went out to the "C" in my imagination, and went to sleep with this image FIXED.

I woke up early and headed out to the car for my trip the airport, and at the last minute, I realized there was something that I had left in my room that really needed to be packed.

I went back into my room to grab the item I required. Then suddenly, I caught something out the corner of my eye.

In the very center of my bed were the wrist weights. In plain sight. My bed was fixed, and I'll be honest, I rarely fix my bed. But, that morning I did.

I am telling you those wrist weights *were not there* when I fixed my bed.

The way they were placed and positioned exactly next to each other for me to see them in the very center of my bed on top of my comforter?!

Again, I was in disbelief.

Then, I heard "Greater things than these…"

> How does this happen?
> Quantum physics.
> How does this happen?
> It is my inheritance. And yours, too.
> We can manifest any "lost item."
> Nothing is lost.

I got in the car for my trip and explained what happened to my kids who were with me. They, too, were excited because they had been looking with me and knew how much I really chose to have them with me on the trip!

> Matthew 17:20 says, "Truly, I tell you, if you have faith as small as a mustard seed, you can say to this mountain "*move from here to there*" and *it will move. Nothing is impossible with God*."

Miracle Example #3

I was hosting a conference locally. My team and I were on the last night of the event. One of my daughters was selling chocolate at the product table throughout the day to support a fundraiser for the school.

She sold all of the chocolate by mid-day and was so proud. She had placed all of the money she earned in her new wallet. It was $40 in total. At 7 years old, $40 may as well have been a BILLION dollars to her.

She went around and told everyone on my team that she had a new wallet and that she had $40! She was soooo proud and excited.

Once the conference was over, we were packing up all the chairs and books and started cleaning up when I saw her at the side of the room crying. I went over to her and said, "Honey, what's wrong?"

She replied, "I lost my wallet! I cannot find it anywhere," with tears in her eyes.

I said, "Honey, first let's change your language... I AM God's eyes seeing my wallet now!" I asked my team to help us look. We looked for a solid hour... all forty of us. When the owner of the building came to lock the doors, it was past midnight. I explained what happened and asked him privately to please be on the lookout for the wallet. He actually started looking at that moment, too. We stayed another 30 minutes looking. There were only two rooms, so there was not a lot of places it could be hiding.

Tired and ready to go, we finally headed to the parking lot. The owner assured me he would keep looking and let me know if he found it. In the parking lot, my daughter was still crying standing next to a lady on my team.

I said to my daughter, "Hey, no worries kiddo! RE-Member when mom couldn't find her wrist weights? I knew exactly where they were! They were on mommy's bed!" I continued, "Let's imagine together that we find the wallet right on the bed."

She lit up! Her face and actually her whole body shifted with the thought. That seemed to help her relax and be excited to go home and see her wallet again.

Now I'll be honest. I did not even BELIEVE what I was saying. I was just trying to help her feel better and stop being so sad.

All 40 of us were heading back to my house for the debrief "after conference" celebration.

When we got back, I immediately went into host mode and was getting out the food and water so everyone could eat. I completely did not even *THINK* about looking for the wallet.

Next thing you know… in walks my daughter, with a full BEAM of DELIGHT and her WALLET IN HAND! All 40 of us were astonished!

I said, "*WHERE* DID YOU FIND IT?"

She said, "When I got home I went straight to your bed, but it was not there. Then I thought, if it's not on your bed maybe it is on MY bed… I ran to my room and there was my wallet sitting in the center of my bed. All the money was inside."

ALL OF US WERE STANDING THERE WITH OUR MOUTHS WIDE OPEN.

Faith like a child. I did not actually believe at this point, **but she did.** She already knew this was possible through *my own testimony.* **The code was tangible for her!** She saw the "C" and Beyond. (RE-Member the timeline code in chapter 12?)

Faith is a powerFULL force energy.

Matthew 18:3 "Truly I tell you, unless you change and become like little children, you will never enter the kingdom of heaven."

That word "kingdom" means, "realm or rule."

The word "heaven" means, "happiness, power, eternity, the heights of the upper regions."

In other words, when we enter with faith like a child, we can enter the portal-door-opportunity for ANYTHING!

This door is our passport to ALL possibilities... all greater things than these.

These type things are NORMAL for anyone awake to participate in. And trust me, these are only the THREE that I mentioned. I have thousands of my own miracles, and those I have worked with have thousands more.

It just takes being awake, RE-Membering LOVE and using the tools available to us.

See the C-D-E-F... Z; be the code of it *already happening* and quantum physics brings the match!

Chapter 21

You Got This!

This is a lot of information to shape your miracle life. Kim Clement[m] used to sing, *"You are somewhere in the future, and you look much better than you look right now!"* I agree. I see you there, or should I say *HERE,* already!

I see you "home." Like I said in the beginning... you have heard the saying "Go big or go home... ?" I say, **"STAY HOME and GO BIG."**

I leave you with a few things.

First:

An encounter/near death experience my mentor and Spiritual Dad, Bob Jones, had one time after physically dying on August 8th, 1976. He said he transmuted to Heaven and saw Light, The Light he knew was God.

God had only one question, "Did you learn to Love?" God asked everyone the same single question. And those who did "learn to love" were let into the heart of God.

God equals Love, Love equals God... He could just as easily have heard the question "Did you learn to God?" I am not saying I am God, or I can be God or that I am above God... I am saying God is in me and

---

m   Kim Clement (1956-2016) was a prophetic minister, author, and international speaker.

nothing can separate me from this Love but my illusion of separation and my will.

God is expecting us to Love and to "God" here as "humans"... Even the word "hu-man" means little God! God wants us to vibrate with the frequency of Love, His frequency, and with that all our abilities are magnified, and we can manifest Divine health, joy and even more LOVE.

Second:

I invite you to practice. Practice staying, practice standing and exercise the spiritual muscle of thinking, feeling, and talking about God and God's Love and all the things Source is in us.

Re-Member the car on top of a hill that's about to coast down, it is much easier to stop the car at the top of the hill while you can, mid-way, or you may just get run over.

Stop all negative thoughts, feelings and words as soon as you can and re-place/re-pent with decrees and new coding and all the things mentioned in the previous chapters.

Even if you screw up, just RE-Pent... and start again. The word Re-Pent means *RE*... to do again and *Pent* as in the Highest Thoughts... the Pent-house. The Master-Mind, HEAD Master, The Mind of Christ. Just go back and RE-set your thoughts on Truth.

I invite you to not just read the words, but apply the practice of what's available to you.

Please know I am your permanent victory in the Light. *Please know I'd love to hear your personal miracles that happen because of this book.*

Lastly, please enjoy these "parting words." It may be the "end" of this book, but I am agreeing that this is only the beginning of creating your new Life of miracles in the C-Z CODE.

I invite you to read this last bit out loud to yourself and your world. Be a "carrier wave" of these words to your realm now and shift.

I AM Love.

I AM Love.

Newton's first law states that *"Every object will remain at rest or in uniform motion in a straight line unless compelled to change its state by the action of an external force…"*

What is the "external force?" Only something we create and/or allow and/or magnetize in, or to, our field.

We can only manifest what we feel and/or what we think on.

We can only draw in what we are.

When I read Newton's first law, *"Every object will remain at rest… unless compelled to change its state…"* I think about our choice to stay or remain in rest, no matter the genetic DNA "pattern/program" or external force or forces we consciously or unconsciously create and "walk out."

In Source and in Rest, we RE-main if we choose.

It is only by compulsion or choice that we engage in split energy.

By choice unconsciously or consciously, we participate in our good and "bad" creations.

Only by conscious awakened choice can we choose Rest over chaos or stress…

Love over fear.

Or, we can choose to permanently stay in Love.

In Source, Psalms 91, our KingDome, we are untouchable.

In Source, Psalms 91, we remain hidden and unaffected by external energy.

We only see Love.

We only notice Love.

We are Love and our Love Stays... a Standing wave.

Even if our hidden unconscious/subconscious fear creates external forces in attempts to split and shift our own path (self-sabotage).

We can choose to stay in Rest in the untouchable of Psalms 91... a single eye.

Ha! We test ourselves?

And even if "outside" external forces come to pursue and persuade.

In Source, nothing negative is allowed. If Love is our standing wave we only match LOVE frequency.

Even if inner DNA genetic conscious or unconscious patterns should arise? We get the choice to BE LOVE.

In Choosing Love, In Source, in Rest, the energy of chaos cannot find us.

And as anything negative looks for access to plug in to stay alive?

There is no opening, no access, no weak-link or sound.

Like a flat wall with no socket. The plug, the cord, and the energy move on looking for a place to land, to connect, to plug in, and stay alive.

"It" requires energy to live and breathe.

We give "it" no energy... no breath, no oxygen.

In Source, we can choose Rest and Love.

In fact, in Source we ARE Love.

We are the INTERNAL and External LOVE Force!

We are Love that compels OTHERS to change their state to RE-Member FULL Love.

In Light, we ARE Light.

In Love, we ARE Love.

We are transformers.

We are converters.

Newton's third law states that, *"For every action (force) in nature, there is an equal and opposite reaction."*

In Source, we stay Love, shifting anything that isn't.

In Source, we stay Love, empowering and reinforcing everything already Loved. (Which is everything and everybody.)

I AM Love.

I was born in Love.

I AM born again and again and AGAIN in Love.

Moment to moment.

In Love, I was created, and I AM continuously created and creating moment to moment IN Love.

I came FROM Love...

IN Love...

TO Love...

FOR Love.

As I Love, I AM Loved.

As I RE-Member Love, others RE-Member Love.

As I Love, I DO WHAT I Love, and I Love what I do.

As I Love and Remain in Love and in Rest, I compel and ignite others to Love.

As I Love and Stay in Love, Love can never be lost Because I AM.

If I look for Love, I will always look for Love. Because Love cannot be found externally.

Love is within.

Love is a choice. Again, and again…

I AM Love. I have always been Love.

My pre-existing condition was Love.

And my current state is Love.

Anything less than Love misses the mark.

Anything less than Love is sin.

All Dis-Ease is forgotten.

In Love All is healing.

In Love ALL is restored and RE-Membered.

Love is The Royal Law.

Love is the highest Law.

The highest Call.

Love is The Door.

The Map.

The Way.

Love is the Code.

Love is the Source.

Love is Pure.

Love is Here. Already. Tangible.

I RE-Member Love Now.

If I look for Love, I will always look for Love. Because "looking for Love" isn't having it. This is word purgatory.

God is Love.

Looking for Love means you are without God or separate from God. This is not true.

God is Love.

God is here. Now.

I AM Love therefore I See Love.

When I RE-Member Love, then, I always have Love.

When I Am Love, Love cannot be "lost."

Because I AM.

This is True. I AM True.

The Word, who is God, Who IS Love, became flesh, and The Word still becomes flesh now today.

Love cannot be found externally. Love is within. I AM Love.

Love is a choice. Again, and again.

I AM Love. And. I. Stay.

Yes, Love is a noun and Love is a verb AND Love is a *Person.*

God /Love In me, to me, through me. Around me.

I AM Love. And Love is me.

Love In me, through me, to me Around me.

I AM Love in motion.

I AM Love in action.

I See Love.

I RE-Member Love.

I Feel Love.

I Do Love.

I Create Love.

I Be Love.

Now.

Endnotes

1. https://www.successconsciousness.com/blog/inner-peace/how-many-tho
    ughts-does-your-mind-think-in-one-hour/.

2. https://medium.com/@igorgurko/three-experiments-that-change-ev-
    erything-2bc578480d34   https://www.societyforunderstanding.co.uk/
    selected-articles/three-experiments-that-change-everything/

    See also: Gregg Braden's book Divine Matrix.

3. https://www.marketplace.org/2017/11/21/tech/inventor-changed-our-
    world-and-also-happened-be-famous-hollywood-star

4. https://chem.libretexts.org/Bookshelves/Physical_and_Theoretical_Che
    mistry_Textbook_Maps/Supplemental_Modules_(Physical_and_
    Theoretical_Chemistry)/Physical_Properties_of_Matter/States_of_
    Matter/Properties_of_Solids/Crystal_Lattice

For more connection to Dr. Sharnael and her powerFULL resources, check out her online bookstore and blog at www.swiftfire.org.

Or connect with her in her other popular classes at www.swiftfire.org/onlineclasses

31 DAYS TO NEW LIFE

DR. SHARNAEL WOLVERTON SEHON, ND

Are you tired of having to lay down on the bed in attempt to zip up your "fat jeans?" Are you absolutely sick and tired of being sick and tired? Take the Keto Reset journey with Dr. Sharnael today! These simple steps will shift your life for the better. Topics include Keto Basics, Keto Sticks, Sugar and your Brain, Energy, Exercise, Intermittent Fasting, Keto and Alcohol, and way more. You won't be sorry. Start now!

AVAILABLE FOR PURCHASE AT SWIFTFIRE.ORG/STORE AND
ALL MAJOR ONLINE RETAILERS

31 DAYS TO NEW LIFE
DR. SHARNAEL WOLVERTON SEHON, ND

START YOUR ONE-YEAR MEMBERSHIP NOW!

✔ Ready to start making wise healthy choices that support divine health?

✔ Ready to do this with LIKE-Minded people all with ONE focus together?

✔ Ready to RE-Member and RE-Mind the brain and body through amazing education/programming and practice?

✔ Ready to see and BE the strong Divine Health that you ARE? Ready to Re-Member and Re-Mind the tools we have to support us daily?

✔ Ready to support the body not just physically and MENTALLY but emotionally? READY TO MAKE THIS FUN AND EASY?

I am hosting a support group full of education, support, programming and FUN to RE-Member and RE-Mind our healthy sugar-free life!

There are 31 videos, articles, recipes, and LITERALLY hundreds of dollars' worth of drawings to keep you in the game. You will have access to these videos and more educational help and support with recipes, fun, tips, interactive support, high energy fellowship of like-minded folks doing this together as one.

AVAILABLE FOR PURCHASE AT:
SWIFTFIRE.ORG/ONLINECLASSES

Crystals, Science and the Bible
with Dr. Sharnael

Interested in more understanding about crystals, oils and science? I have a special *Interactive* Private Facebook Membership Class and Group!

✔ Classes and Interviews
✔ 100's of educational posts
✔ How do Oils and Crystals work together?
✔ Fun high-vibe community for Truth finders
✔ Tips and Testimonies from others on the journey
✔ One-year membership to enjoy ongoing videos, classes, and educational posts

Meet others on the same path, all interacting and Re-Membering together! Joins us today!

Use Discount code "CrystalDeal4U" as my personal thank you!

Check out swiftfire.org/onlineclasses to find the Online Class section.

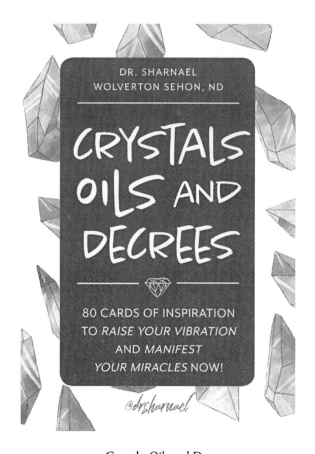

Crystals, Oils and Decrees

80 Cards of Inspiration to Raise your Vibration and Manifest your Miracles Now!

AVAILABLE FOR PURCHASE AT:
SWIFTFIRE.ORG/STORE